WHERE HAS MY LITTLE GIRL GONE?

*How to protect your daughter
from growing up too soon*

A Lion Book
an imprint of
Lion Hudson plc
Wilkinson House, Jordan Hill Road,
Oxford OX2 8DR, England
www.lionhudson.com
ISBN 978 0 7459 5542 1

Distributed by:
UK: Marston Book Services, PO Box 269, Abingdon, Oxon,
OX14 4YN
USA: Trafalgar Square Publishing, 814 N. Franklin Street,
Chicago, IL 60610
USA Christian Market: Kregel Publications, PO Box 2607,
Grand Rapids, Mn 49501

First edition 2011
10 9 8 7 6 5 4 3 2 1 0

Typeset in 11/13 Times (TT)
Printed in Great Britain by Clays Ltd, St Ives plc

Please note that the names of the daughters and mothers
interviewed in the plastic surgery clinic and by
Childline have been changed to protect their privacy.

Contents

PART **3**

Growing up in the X-rated society   86

Introduction

Missbimbo.com, a website popular with children, calls itself "a place where bimbos from around the world can join one another and be proud and happy of Bimboland". Here, girls of any age control their virtual characters, who start off with an ideal weight of 127 lbs and an IQ of 70. A player must work on getting herself either a hot boyfriend to increase her street cred, or a rich one to boost her bank balance. At any one time there are thousands of "bimbos" online – in all more than 2.5 million registered users.

After the Hollywood star Tom Cruise's daughter Suri was seen wearing high heels at the age of three, high-street giant Next insisted it was proud to sell similar styles to nursery-school age girls. A spokesman said: "Their popularity suggests many parents agree we've come up with a look that's special without seeming inappropriately grown up."[1]

Sasha Bennington, 13, is one of the most successful child beauty queens in the UK, which now has twenty contests for kids. She undergoes an intensive beauty routine including a weekly spray tan, new acrylic nails each month, and regular highlights. Her mother, Jayne, a former model, says: "We spend about £300 a month on beauty treatments for her. Sasha's friends are the same. All girls their age are. Why else would you be able to buy make-up for pre-teens at Boots?" Asked how she sees herself, Sasha says: "Blonde, pretty, dumb – I don't need brains."[2]

In our house, there is always one four-letter word which is expressly forbidden: D.I.E.T. Ever since I interviewed the mother of an anorexic six-year-old and heard how her daughter wanted to be slim like the models she saw in magazines, I made a point of not so much as uttering it within earshot of my two young daughters. If other adults brought up the subject of their own diet regimes within my children's hearing, I discreetly changed the subject, lest impressionable ears soak up the idea that it's a woman's lot to constantly starve herself.

Because I wanted Lily and Clio to have a real childhood, I carefully monitored what they both watched on television, where they went on the internet, and what magazines were left around the house. So it came as a shock when Lily, then aged seven, came home and told me she was on a diet because one of her friends had told her she was fat – and during the floods of tears that followed, Clio, then three, duly piped up: "Yes, thin means you're perfect!"

Looking back, maybe I should have spotted the signs earlier. After Christmas, Lily started doing press-ups and skipping on the spot. I thought it was just a youthful excess of energy – although I was baffled as to why she would stop and ask me if she looked any different. I also noticed she refused sugar on her cereal, but it didn't worry me unduly. Finally, after several days of this behaviour, she tearfully approached me in the kitchen and asked for a hug. Then it all came tumbling out. In the course of a quarrel, one of her friends had called her the most feared word in her playground: "fat".

First my mind went blank. Then I felt as though I was stepping into a minefield. I looked her in the eye and told her she was absolutely right for her height and age. Privately, though, I knew what the issue was. It was true that Lily still had not grown out of the soft roundness of her toddler years, while her friends now had the sparrow-like limbs of middle childhood. It was a shock because I had always tried to instil a love and acceptance of how she looked – and never criticized or commented.

In the days that followed, it was clear that my assurances had not been heard – and that peer pressure and creeping expectations that girls should look a certain way held much more sway. Despite my best efforts to protect her, Lily was being fast-tracked through childhood. How did she even know about calories – or that sugar was full of them? I started to wonder if, instead of playing hopscotch, she and her friends were swapping diet tips at playtime.

Like many other concerned parents, I was already aware that something was going badly wrong for our daughters because of the way girls grow up too fast. Indeed, in study after study, in societies all over the Western world – the United States, Australia, Holland, and the UK – the issue had been identified and analysed in great depth. *Yet for all the extensive research – and the quickening pace of government towards regulating the media, marketers, and the internet – I found very little which actually told parents themselves how to protect their girls.*

Now that Lily's childhood was under siege, I didn't know what to say or do to stop these messages reaching her at this critical time in her development, or where to turn for help. My experience was a stark warning that it wasn't going to be possible to shield my girls completely – and a reminder that once gone, innocence is lost forever. But as a journalist and a writer on parenting, I found it unthinkable that parents should have to sit powerlessly on the sidelines while marketers and the media eroded our girls' childhoods. Over the next two years, I interviewed psychologists, parenting educators, teachers, and more than eighty families to try to find the best way forward. I started off not knowing if there even was an answer. But gradually I found a growing consensus.

Until sexualizing children becomes socially unacceptable once again, there is no use in trying to lock our children away, like Rapunzel in the tower. Like many parents, that had been my initial instinct. But sexualization is already in the air our daughters breathe. While regulation of the media would certainly help, the most important steps need to be taken by individuals: we must look within ourselves, support our daughters, and offer them not only insights, but also alternatives.

That's why this book takes a three-pronged approach.

So that we start off from the best possible position to protect our girls, the first section of the book deals with how to organize our own attitudes and ideas, so that the conscious and unconscious messages we send to our girls are healthy, clear, and consistent.

The second section looks at how, by building self-esteem in our children, we can go some way towards inoculating them against the worst effects of the influences they encounter. If we can create a strong core of self-belief during our girls' formative years, they will be more able to stand firm against the pressure to reduce themselves to nothing more than the sum of their physical features. By really opening up channels of communication in the "tween" years, we have a chance of staying closer to them when the going really gets tough – and of showing them how to reject those influences.

The third section looks at society through the eyes of our children. It thinks about how they see it, and how we need to help them learn for themselves to discern what's good and bad. This section offers lots of practical ways we can help to tone down, if not turn off, the effects of raunch culture.

None of this can happen overnight. The sooner we begin with our girls, the better. There is no quick fix. The "tween" years in particular – the ages between around seven and twelve – are a critical period when parents can help girls develop an unassailable sense of self. It's during this period that our power to influence positively is also at its peak, before the inevitable separation of adolescence means that our daughters' peers begin to drown us out. If we really work at staying connected to our girls in those years, we have a better chance of being able to guide them when things get tough.

If we succeed, our daughters are less likely to degrade or sacrifice any part of themselves when the pressure to be "sexy" really piles on in their teenage years. But all is not lost if we miss that opportunity. Just by becoming a more aware parent today, you can help make your daughter more media and emotionally literate. In the two minutes you take to show her how a magazine photograph of an ultra-skinny, perfect model has been airbrushed, you have taught her not to hold herself up against an ideal that doesn't exist. By talking about and explaining what's happening around her today, you can help to shelter her against the drip, drip, drip erosion of her self-worth. Because it's such a huge problem, this book offers hundreds of suggestions to parents. It would be impossible to put them all into practice: you know your daughter best, and you need to pick the ones that will work for you and your family.

Yes, parts of this book will be upsetting. Facing up to what's out there and making our girls resilient and strong isn't going to be easy. You may also have to look at yourself to see whether the creeping sexualization of society has affected your values too. But if this helps your daughter be a little more true to herself, rather than feeling she has to fit into today's stifling stereotypes of good looks and "sexiness", we will have won back some of her freedom to live without these constraints. If we don't succeed, the price is high for our girls. A rise in eating disorders, self-harm, depression, casual and meaningless sex, teenage pregnancy and under-age drinking is a side-effect when girls judge themselves only by their appearance and their sexual experience.

Ultimately the mental health – the happiness – of our children is at stake. One in ten children in the UK suffers some form of mental illness according to recent official estimates.[3] More than a quarter of children say that they "often feel depressed" – and the thing that makes girls most unhappy is how they look. It's heartbreaking that as early as nine and ten our daughters are already judging themselves as losers in the beauty contest of life.[4]

As a mother of two girls, I am writing this book because I do not want my children, despite all their accomplishments and wonders, to be judged solely on how they look. I am worried about my daughters growing up in a culture in which sex is never called "making love" any more. At the very best, it's called "sex" – or in the pornography from which it has become impossible to shield our children, it's called "pounding" or "slamming".

Although this would be the subject of another book, boys are also becoming victims of the sexualized society: they face increasing pressure to act like porn stars and look like male models. So I am also writing this because I fear for my daughters' relationships with men they have not yet met, and who may be being imprinted with pornographic images which portray women as "whores" and "sluts" with whom men can't form real relationships.

My daughters don't deserve this – and neither do yours.

PART 1

"Mum, Dad, can I have a nose job, please?" The rise of the X-Factor parent

It's just after 10.00 a.m. in Harley Street, and the doors have opened at one of London's larger plastic surgery clinics. At reception, patients are being greeted by a rank of identikit receptionists in black suits and red lipstick. Now, dotted around the beige soft furnishings, the first intake of customers is busy leafing through a stack of celebrity magazines. My job this morning is to ask them why they are here.

The number of people undergoing plastic surgery in the UK is rising at the fastest rate in history. According to Mintel, the market for cosmetic surgery has grown in the last two years alone by 17 per cent, and is now worth an estimated 2.3 billion pounds.[5] So why exactly has the need to look "perfect" become such an epidemic – and how, at a time of economic recession and high unemployment, do people find the money? As I looked around the waiting room as it began to fill, it was striking to see that many of the women there were in their late teens or early twenties.

Flawlessly made up and doe-eyed, Amelie has the petite face and body of a young Audrey Hepburn – and the pert breasts, outlined by a skin-tight black T-shirt, of a glamour model. In fact, she works as a cosmetics sales assistant in a nearby department store, and she is back for a post-operative review after getting her 32-inch chest boosted two cup sizes, "for confidence". The £4,500 cost of the operation is probably not far off a quarter of her yearly take-home salary. But like so many of her generation, who can't afford to move out, Amelie lives at home – and anyway her mum and dad paid for the surgery. "I told them I wanted them done and they said: 'OK, if that's what you want,'" she explains matter-of-factly, as if her parents were giving her the down-payment on her first car. "They didn't worry. They said: 'If it makes you feel better about yourself, then that's fine.'"

In the other corner of the room, I approach twenty-year-old Elaine. With her tongue stud and skinny jeans tucked into Ugg boots, Elaine looks more like an off-duty member of Girls Aloud than the legal secretary she is. She recently had a nose job, once again paid for in part by a loan from the bank of mum and dad. "I know it's going to sound really funny, but there was nothing wrong with my old nose," she insists. "It just looked a bit funny in pictures. My friend had it done when she was eighteen. Plus everyone's doing it. Surgery is getting younger these days. Six of my friends have had boob jobs. One went up to a double F and she loves all the men paying her attention. As soon as you find out from your friends that it doesn't hurt that much, there's nothing to stop you. The moment I woke up from my nose job, I asked about a boob job – and I'm still thinking about it."

Because it's her first session, Courtney, who is eighteen, is being accompanied by her mother this morning. They have travelled from Kent to start a course of £1,200 laser treatments to get rid of stretch marks. Like the others, flawlessly made up, and a size 6 in skinny jeans and a T-shirt which is cut away to reveal her tiny waist, Courtney continually smoothes down her waterfall of glossy auburn hair. As if she is about to be cured of a life-threatening disease, Courtney explains that she developed "terrible red lines" across her tummy and thighs when she put on two stone after starting the contraceptive pill. Now, with just a few months to go before the start of a performing arts course, both mum and daughter are frantically trying to get rid of them for fear they should stand in the way of her career.

Once she's gone in for her treatment, Courtney's mother, Justine, confides why, as a responsible parent, she felt she had no choice but to do something. "It's true the treatments are quite expensive. But what choice have you got when something like this is ruining your daughter's life? It's wrecked her social life. When her friends ring her and ask her to join them on sleepovers, she says no because she can't bear anyone to see her in her underwear. I saw her sitting there with the tears streaming down her face. It was heart-breaking. She kept saying: 'Why has this happened to me, Mum? How could this happen to me?'"

Louise, a student, is also here because of her parents' generosity, although with only the tiniest bump on her nose, it's hard to foresee how her life will change after rhinoplasty. But her elder sister had already been treated to surgery by their parents to tidy up some loose skin after losing weight. In order to be absolutely fair, her parents told her that she could think of something to have done too.

It was just a snapshot. But as I interviewed more girls during my research for this book, I found almost every young woman seemed to have a notional shopping list of faults she felt she had to get "fixed". The result is that market researchers now consider young people to be the main growth market for plastic surgery. In the last two years alone, the number of young people considering such surgery has risen more sharply than that for any other age group. Almost six out of ten people between the ages of sixteen and twenty-four – young people in the prime of their looks and attractiveness – now want surgery to improve or "correct" their appearance, double the number for people over fifty-five. The only thing that stands in their way is money – but with parents increasingly willing to foot the bill, that's becoming less of a barrier to "fixing" what they believe is wrong with them. [6]

Of course, it's painful for a parent to witness the anxieties teenage girls go through about their looks. But what was sobering was the quality of the reasons these young women had for choosing cosmetic surgery. As I remembered, such surgery used to be undertaken to fix flaws that caused crippling insecurities and unhappiness. Yet the most common explanations I heard were that their friends had had something done too, that they wanted to look better in pictures – or just because they could.

None cited celebrity culture as a factor. But then it's so pervasive and ingrained that most girls growing up today have never known any other ideal but perfection. Most learned about makeovers from TV shows at their mothers' knees. And what surprised me was how many parents, far from trying to talk their girls out of it, or trying to put these concerns in perspective, were prepared to foot the bill. Whatever objections they raised in private or in the run-up to the operations (to which I was not privy) they still handed over their credit cards. Like the mentors on X-factor, in the final analysis they went along with the belief that a perfect cookie cutter appearance – here achieved by cosmetic enhancement – is what a modern girl needs to get on in life.

With younger girls, a similar trend is reflected in the rise of child beauty contests. In the mid-2000s, there were no such contests in Britain. In 2010 there were more than twenty, thanks, in part, to the instant fame of reality television stars and the luxurious lifestyles of glamour models. More than 12,000 girls are entered into the Miss Teen Queen UK competition each year. Yet none of this would be happening without the drive and the cash of parents behind it.[7]

X-factor parenting is also filtering down to our schools where "prom nights" are being laid on for children as young as seven, for which proud mums and dads fork out small fortunes on make-up artists, Barbie-doll ball dresses, and limos. So widespread is the trend that prom companies now tour Britain's schools handing out flyers for local beauty treatments including hair extensions and spray-on tans.[8]

For more specific evidence of the slippery slope we put our children on if we allow them to believe that looks are what count most, then we need look no further than the example of Sophie Watson. At fourteen, Sophie was allowed by her mother, Joy Watson-Carr, to have £1,000 worth of semi-permanent make-up tattooed onto her face to fill out her lips and eyebrows. As Sophie told GMTV – as well as a wide range of other national media – she had no terrible deformities or insecurities that needed correcting. "I saw it on TV and quite a few celebs have got it done... There was nothing wrong with my face. I was happy with it. I just decided I wanted to enhance my natural features a bit more."[9] Joy, a beauty therapist who has also had her eyebrows tattooed on, says: "I was happy for her to have it done. We talked about it for a long time. There aren't many fourteen-year-olds who don't experiment with hair dye and make-up. It's just part of growing up. She wanted it done, so I said yes."

Sophie started modelling at the age of eleven, dressed in floaty princess dresses. Now, still aged only fourteen, her recent photo shoots show how far she is prepared to go to maintain the attention. The pictures show her in high heels, a bra, and a thong, kneeling on a bed. Others show her posing uncomfortably in a range of pink lacy and sequinned underwear sets, and pulling down the waistband of her buttock-skimming shorts like a porn star in training. In an interview that Joy gave three months after the permanent make-up episode she reveals that her daughter lost her virginity a week after her fourteenth birthday, has started drinking heavily, and has been in trouble at school for flouting uniform and make-up rules.[10]

It would be unfair to single out Joy too much. Despite how her values are affecting her daughter, like every mother she genuinely believes she is doing the right thing to help her child get on in life. Indeed, most weeks there are new stories in the press about mothers who give their pre-teenage children Botox to "keep wrinkles at bay", or who are putting six-year-olds on strict calorie controlled diets, lest they also lose out in life. They are now so plentiful, the only surprise is that they remain newsworthy.

These are, of course, extreme examples that few parents reading this book would identify with. But just as I had to look more closely at my values when my daughter put herself on a diet – and examine whether my good-intentioned references to "healthy foods" and my regular gym dates had sent her skewed messages – it helps to go back to the source.

Take yourself back to the moment you knew you were having a baby girl. Was your first thought to imagine how pretty she was going to be, or the lovely dresses you were going to put her in? If you're also the parent of a son, ask yourself if that's also how you felt when you learned you were having a boy. Would it be fair to say that his outfits and how handsome he might be were lower on your list of priorities?

It's a tough lesson, but if we are going to fight against our girls being judged on how they look, we have to start thinking about our own expectations and how they have been shaped in us over the last twenty or thirty years. After all, if we were born during or after the 1960s, we were the first generation to grow up in a world dominated by television. With TV becoming our main national pastime, as children we quickly picked up that, for a woman, being thin and beautiful equals sexy and successful. Our generation has seen the rise of reality TV stars, WAGs, and manufactured girl bands who have collectively sent the message that you can be rich and famous without talent. Pretty and pushy is all you need.

As these celebrities have attracted continuous attention and amassed impressive wealth, and as reality TV has made these things seem to be within the grasp of everybody, have we not also signed up to the idea that females need to look a certain way to get on in life? Without realizing it, have we also come to covet a celebrity lifestyle and appearance for our own children? Of course, through the ages, parents have always prized their daughters' attractiveness. The faces of our children – their smooth skin, shiny hair, large eyes, and soft features – are the prototype for adult perfection, and little girls are, by their very nature, beautiful.

This is a particularly difficult area for parents because we are damned if we don't address appearance with our girls – and damned if we do. With the best will in the world, we can't pretend that looks don't matter one bit. Girls are so acutely sensitive that those whose parents never mention their looks assume it is because they are ugly. So simply not attaching any importance to appearance whatsoever is not the answer. It's *how much* importance we attach to beauty in a society already obsessed by looks, in which everyone is measured on a sliding scale of perfection, that is now key.

So while, as parents, we are entitled to prize beauty, in this hyper-sexualized age we have to try our best not to fall in with the general trend of treating it as the most important quality our girls have. We need to make it clear that their looks are a small part of what they are – not *who* they are. Starting early in their lives, it's vital to prize other values – such as kindness, honesty, generosity, self-awareness, and self-acceptance – that have been drowned out by a culture of superficiality. Rather than encouraging the draw towards celebrity and consumerism, we need to divert them away from the identikit ideal of feminine attractiveness – perma tanned skin, poker straight hair, and a size 8 body – towards valuing qualities which are not visible. Because if, as their most important role models, we endorse society's message that looks are the most important thing about them, we don't equip our children for success. In fact we set them up for failure, dissatisfaction, and unhappiness with themselves. We don't allow them to develop their inner life. Instead we let them drift towards becoming empty-headed, celebrity clones.

Why parents feel powerless

Being a parent of girls is already a tough job. But it's even tougher for the families of today who are trying to screen out more negative influences than ever before on their daughters' healthy development. Compare, for a moment, the influences on your own childhood with those on your daughter's.

The internet has only become generally available in the last fifteen years, with broadband only making it an ever-present fact of life in maybe the last six or seven. Probably, during your own childhood, if you watched TV alone it was mainly in the prescribed after-school period, or on Saturday morning, when there were shows created for kids your age. Certainly when I was growing up in the 1970s our family had just one TV, and we would all gather round to watch light entertainment programmes designed for everyone, such as *This is Your Life* or *The Morecambe and Wise Show*.

True, there was sexism – much of it a spill-over from the *Carry On* humour of the 1960s – in programmes such as *The Benny Hill Show*. Some television showed women as passive sex objects, such as *Miss World*. Still, the only place you could be guaranteed to see a topless woman was not on TV, but on page three of *The Sun*. And though it may have been implied, there wasn't much sex – certainly nothing of the intensity we have now. Anything much stronger than a kiss or a mild swear-word was unheard of before the 9.00 p.m. watershed. Compared with children growing up today, our childhoods were androgynous. But because it's all happened relatively quickly, it's hard for us as parents to take on what our daughters' childhoods are like – and how overwhelming the world can seem from their very innocent point of view.

With sex and body image now so deeply woven into the fabric of music, advertising, TV, magazines, fashion, and the internet it's understandable that many parents already feel defeated. They feel society has moved on and that this is a fact we have to live with. The families I spoke to handled creeping sexualization in a variety of ways. Generally, they fell into a range between prohibitive – insisting they could screen out everything – and permissive – believing they had no choice but to go along with it.

Before we start looking at where we need to go from here, it may be worthwhile considering where we, as parents, are starting from. Do any of these beliefs match your own?

"There's nothing we can do – so why try?"

Among the many parents I interviewed for this book, there was a real sense of fear and powerlessness. Many had taken the route of weary surrender. "There's nothing we can do" was a common refrain. Mothers and fathers told me they didn't know where to start because the media seemed too vast and out of control. After all, with something as huge as the world wide web, to whom do you complain? These parents felt drowned out as advertisers, retailers, broadcasters, and negative peer pressure overwhelmed their influence. According to a 2010 Mothers' Union survey of 1,000 parents of children aged under eighteen, one in five parents feel they have no control over what their children see on the internet any more. The same proportion also feel they have lost control over what their children do on social networking sites.[11]

Parents in this category often start off being restrictive, but panic once they realize the influences of sexualization seem beyond their control. But it's far too soon – and far too dangerous – to fall into a state of paralysis. While it's true that we can't shield our children, we can inoculate them against the effects of what they see by explaining, appropriately for their age, what is happening all around them. By helping girls to question the pressures placed on them, we really can help them work out for themselves what is good and bad for them.

Furthermore, far from being impotent, parents remain a powerful force. While corporations do like profits, they also hate bad publicity. So although businesses may sometimes court notoriety by pushing boundaries, thankfully exploiting children is still a taboo with which no respectable company wants to be associated. Parents need to point out when the boundaries are being pushed too far, so that the taboo remains in place.

It took just one mother, Nikola Evans, to get Asda to apologize for and withdraw a display of padded bras for girls as young as nine from an aisle at their Sheffield store. Following a national outcry from parents and campaigners, Primark also removed padded bras for seven-year-olds from its shelves, while Tesco stopped selling toy pole-dancing kits.[12]

Advertising, TV, and other areas of the media also have complaints bodies, but they are sadly underused. All it usually takes is a single complaint to launch an investigation and move society an inch closer to being more conscious of and accountable for the welfare of girls.

"If I just say no, it won't happen to my child."

Early in our daughters' childhoods, when they are still babies and toddlers, it's reassuring to tell ourselves that if we don't buy them Bratz dolls, park them in front of the internet or computer games for hours, or dress them in T-shirts with slogans such as "So many boys, so little time", we can protect them from sexualization. But sexualization is not a tap you switch off. It's more like gas that filters through the gaps no matter how many wet towels you press under the doorframe.

As your daughter gets older, peer pressure will play an increasingly large part in the decisions she makes. And if we try to prevent our girls from ever seeing or hearing negative influences, they will never get the chance to work out for themselves how to spot – or cope with – the dangers. We also risk their becoming so intrigued that, once they are out of our control, they become eager to try everything we've attempted to keep them away from.

Most of all, children need to learn to judge for themselves. Ultimately, it's more realistic to equip your child and warn her what's coming. Explain where the pressures come from and the commercial realities behind them. Explain that marketers target young girls because they are the most innocent consumers, and that ads only work by playing on girls' insecurities and desire to fit in.

Make it an ongoing conversation. Help her to see the bigger picture. By decoding what is going on around her as she experiences it, you will be equipping her with a virtual gas mask that can help her filter out the toxic fumes.

"I don't want to tell her anything because it will take away her innocence."

Many parents also feel confused and panicky about how much information to give to forewarn their children. They feel afraid of robbing their daughters of their innocence by telling them about the pressures they might come under. These are parents who may find it painful to acknowledge when their daughters are ready to start learning more about sex. I spoke to many mums who were uncomfortable about sex education classes, even in Year Five (around the age of ten), because they preferred to believe there was no need for them.

The risk of such attitudes is that if we don't tell children about sex, then the internet will get there first – and sooner than we think. If our girls do end up learning about sex, as so many do, by stumbling across pornography, this is going to be as far as possible from the healthy messages we want to give them.

Talking to your children about sex won't encourage them to go and do it. Quite the opposite. More than 250 studies have found that the best way to protect girls against early sexual behaviour is to make sure they are responsibly informed about sex in the first place.[13] Frightening though this may feel, there really are always warm, non-scary ways to talk about it. But don't keep preparing yourself for a big "birds and bees" chat that never quite happens. Make it an ongoing conversation with your daughter, and add more detail as and when she needs it. Let her know that sex should have context and meaning. Parents need to accept that this is a conversation that may feel strange to start with. Few of us like the idea of our little girl growing up and becoming sexual. But accept rather than deny what's happening, because it will happen whether you want it to or not. Once you get going, you may even warm to the subject – although don't tell her more than she needs or you will end up confusing her. We won't be with our daughter when she makes her sexual choices, but if we've talked her through them, she's likely to make safer, more meaningful ones.

"My daughter's a good girl. She's not interested."

This was a common refrain among the parents I interviewed. In fact, very few of them – even those with older girls – were aware of their children seeing sexual or pornographic images except as a one-off or completely by accident. The fact that girls are excellent keepers of secrets helps parents live in this bubble.

Among the many studies to paint a rather different picture is a 2005 report from the London School of Economics, which found that, while 57 per cent of children between the ages of nine and nineteen had seen pornography, only 16 per cent of their parents knew. When it comes to knowing whether or not their daughters are having sex, parents are also wide of the mark. Studies have found that in 50 per cent of cases, mums and dads who believed their children were virgins were wrong.[14]

Many wealthier, middle-class parents often prefer to believe that sexual content in the media is not a threat to their children – as if it was something that didn't affect their children. But in fact middle-class children are more exposed because they more often have their own computers, and tend to navigate further and more skilfully around the internet. The 2005 study also found that middle-class children spent more time on the internet, and had better online skills – and were therefore more successful at evading parental monitoring should they wish to.

So, be realistic. Difficult though it can be to face up to, you'll be in a stronger position if you accept your children as sexual beings rather than avoiding the uncomfortable truth that they are.

"Everyone else's kids are doing it – so mine will just learn from them."

Some parents feel that, however much they protect their girls, they will just learn from their peers at school anyway, so what's the point? Others say they don't speak up about things they disapprove of because other parents aren't saying much either. Underlying this is the worry that they won't look "cool" if they are the only ones who don't let their daughters sign up to Facebook, go to nightclubs, or see films that they're legally too young for. But just as you hope that your child will stand up to peer-group pressure, it's important you do the same.

Make your own decisions. It takes a strong parent to say no when most of the others are saying yes. I know of one mother who vetoed a plan by a group of other mothers to have a "makeover tent" at their primary school fête. She says they now ignore her – but she's impervious because she truly believes she did the right thing for her nine-year-old daughter.

When it comes to conflicts with other parents, what's more important? The fact that, at worst, you might be viewed as the kill-joy at the school gates – or protecting your child and perhaps helping other parents be more conscious of the messages they are sending out? Don't let other parents decide how fast your child grows up because you don't want to stick out. Apart from anything else, you will also be setting a good example to your daughter by standing up for what you believe in.

"I think it's a good thing."

Some parents actively enjoy the fact that their children grow up fast. They see it as a sign that their children are more sophisticated than others, and as a reflection of their own ability to move with the times. Some may also believe it makes them look like cooler parents, and enjoy the popularity with their children's peers that comes with being the most permissive parents in their daughter's circle.

Mums who think they married well owing to their own good looks – or who feel insecure about the lack of them – may also find it flattering and amusing to hear their daughters called "hot" as early as nine or ten and are happy to share the credit. There may also be parents who created an impression at school by being the first to do things such as lose their virginity. Equally, they may have felt ignored or slighted by the opposite sex at the same age, and don't want the same thing to happen to their own girls.

But children are not competing in a race to sexual competence, and they are living their childhoods, not yours. Ask yourself: what exactly is the rush? Sex can only distract them during a crucial period in their education and development. They have the rest of their lives. Just because your daughter looks grown up and "sexy" doesn't mean she is inside. She is more fragile than you think.

"We did it all in my day."

Other parents dismiss sexualization by saying that every generation is shocked by what the younger generation does. "We did all that in our day," they say. "We went out with boys and drank and smoked – and we turned out OK, didn't we?" These parents argue that little girls have always wanted to look older and tried on their mums' high heels – and it didn't do them any harm.

Indeed, but the stakes have got much higher. While we may all remember rolling up our skirts the moment the school bell rang, did we really dress to look like strippers? And we might have looked a couple of years older than we were at twelve, but did we really look eighteen? Furthermore, the pornography we may have seen – after a lot of effort and subterfuge – would have been the soft-core variety showing women in various stages of undress, not the hard-core kind that is now the only material you see on the web.

Yes, your parents' childhood would also have seemed old-fashioned compared with your own. But your daughter's childhood has now been fast-forwarded out of all recognition. Advances in technology – gadgets, phones, broadband, and the rest – have happened in the last decade at a dizzying rate. In any other period of history, our children – and we – would have had time to adjust and get used to them. Our girls are at risk because of the gulf that has opened up between our understanding of technology – and theirs. Because we didn't realize how quickly it was happening, we got left behind. We are only now starting to catch up, as the full effects have become obvious.

"We believe in free speech and modern technology."

Those of us who grew up after the 1960s like the idea of appearing "cool" to our children. The image of the 1950s buttoned-up dad with his pipe and slippers, and the mum with a perm and an apron still casts a long shadow. No one wants to be cast in the role of the blue-rinsed spoil-sport like Mary Whitehouse, scandalized by today's youth, especially as such attitudes have come to be identified with the right wing and religious fundamentalism.

Many mothers I spoke to were also afraid of raising their concerns because they didn't want to appear "politically incorrect". They felt that other mothers would think they were over-reacting if they complained about sexist attitudes in school – or they would be unpopular with teachers for being "trouble makers". But by standing back and not getting involved because we are worried about how we might look we allow control of the situation to slip from our grasp.

It is our failure to challenge the culture that created these problems that allows the internet to be almost completely unregulated in the name of "free speech", so that pornography has become one of its main preoccupations. The question we must ask is: who is benefiting from this freedom – and who is really paying the price?

"They'll do it anyway."

Yes, I am afraid that, hard though it may be to admit, eventually our daughters will end up having sex. But hopefully that day will come later – and at a time when they are emotionally ready. No one wants their daughter to be one of the one in three who lose their virginity on a one-night stand, or of the 50 per cent who say it happened when they were drunk. The right time will come when your daughter is in a meaningful relationship in which she wants to express her trust and love – and not when her friends are daring her, or because she feels she needs to keep up with them.

If a teenage girl is really determined to have sex, there's realistically not much that her parents can do to stop it. Somehow and sometime she will make it happen. But we can do our best to arm our girls so that pornography or peer pressure don't influence that decision.

Don't make children the butt of our jokes

Somewhere along the way it became cute and funny to make children into mini-adults. On the market now, for example, are baby-grows for newborn girls with messages such as "Sorry, I only date rock-stars" and tops for babies with nipple tassels on the front. It's almost as if it's all right for us to have a good laugh at the expense of their innocence – as long as our children don't get the joke.

This probably started with Hollywood films aimed at children, but which were meant to keep the parents amused at the same time. Scripts are often littered with double-entendres that are expected to entertain adults but go over the heads of children in the audience. Recently I attended the afternoon children's show at a family hotel during the Easter half-term with my two girls. Instead of producing a line of bunting from a small boy's T-shirt, in the time-honoured fashion, the conjuror produced several bras tied together. He had meant to play to the grown-ups in the room – and raised a small titter. Meanwhile the child looked confused and deeply embarrassed. But at the risk of sounding humourless, how can we redraw the boundaries around our children's childhoods if we keep making them a laughing matter? Our children deserve better than to be the butt of our jokes.

The "tween" years: the crucial window

The tween years are often seen as the lull before the storm in child development. Although this book is written for parents of girls of all ages, it's worth pointing out that this is when we can make the most positive impact. The ages between seven and twelve are a critical period in your daughter's development. The philosopher Rudolf Steiner once described these middle years as the "root of childhood". If you look back at your own life, they are probably the years you remember as your "childhood".

During this period, your daughter is just starting to define herself as a separate person away from you, her parents. She will become more curious about the world around her and her own place in it. It's during this time that your daughter will form the foundations of her self-image and self-esteem – and it's now that you can help her build herself up. But because girls this age are so open, they are also very vulnerable. That's why they need time to think, to day-dream, and to work out for themselves where they fit in – free from any stereotype of what it means to be female and without being jolted into prematurely sexual roles. They need time to breathe before the ego-challenging pressures of sex and courtship start to kick in. Ideally, they can just be themselves.

For now, parents still remain the major influence in a girl's life. This is a time when our daughters will look to us as role models, and see our values in practice and take them on board. Before too long, as they move into the more challenging teenage years, part of growing up means they will turn away from their families and start listening more to their friends. Of course it's never too early – or too late – to start. Every stage is important. It's as critical to protect and nurture a three-year-old as it is a thirteen-year-old. But if we are conscious of our role as parents during the tween years, our voice will be heard most clearly.

How we talk to our girls

Even in the most loving families, an amazing amount of sexual stereotyping takes place. Some of it is conscious – but much of it unconscious. Parents diminish their girls by referring to them as "little dolls", "poppets", and "minxes", or by treating them as frail little sparrows in need of protection. As parents we need to choose our words carefully, and think how they resonate in our daughters' minds.

As Dr Linda Papadopoulos found during her research for the Home Office Review into the sexualization of children, the word "sexy" is now being used as an expression of approval – even by mothers about their daughters. Do we really want our girls to feel they have to live up to this type of praise? We need to look deeply into ourselves to recognize that we may be sending complex and contradictory messages to our girls. Why, on the one hand, are we encouraging them to believe they are as smart and competent as boys, but then undermining them, on the other, with the idea that they are weak and defenceless? Choose your words to make your daughter feel strong and independent, not weak and in need of male admiration and protection.

What mothers can do

At the age of seven, Poppy Burge is already following in her mum's footsteps. Mother-of-three Sarah first spotted her daughter's "flare" for pole-dancing when she was four and started imitating the dance routines of her idol, Miley Cyrus. As a former Playboy bunny, Sarah is in a good position to help her daughter sharpen her skills, with weekly lessons at home.[15] While she has her critics, Sarah is fiercely proud that there are no lengths to which she will not go to improve her daughter's chances in life. Pole-dancing is good exercise, she insists, and practising dance routines to Britney Spears' "Baby One More Time" does Poppy no more harm than hanging off a climbing frame. "Poppy is very mature for her age and acts like a mini adult," explains Sarah. "She already wears heels, make-up, and designer clothes... She takes at least an hour to get ready for her lesson and is never without her lip gloss."

With blonde hair extensions and heavy eye make-up, Sarah also takes a lot of care with her appearance. She often goes away for a few days to get herself tweaked and improved, and has spent tens of thousands on cosmetic procedures. Poppy is catching on fast. After all, she is learning at her mother's knee. When Sarah recently got another top-up of Botox she asked, "Mummy, are you making your wrinkles go away?" The Year Two pupil has also observed that her mother's breasts have been enhanced by cosmetic surgery – and has since expressed an interest in having hers done when they grow.

As a mother, Sarah is an extreme example. And, like most mothers, she honestly believes she has her child's best interests at heart. Yet part of the reason that so many girls are unhappy is that their mothers set them on a path of endless dissatisfaction through their own never-ending quest for perfection. Just 2 per cent of adult women feel that they are beautiful, according to *The Real Truth About Beauty: A Global Report*.[16] That leaves a huge 98 per cent who feel they are not – and a lot of little girls observing their mummies' ongoing unhappiness with the way they look. The cult of youth means that most of us spend a lot of time and money trying to look younger. As our girls turn into teenagers, and try to look older, everyone seems to be heading into an elusive no-man's-land of perfection somewhere in the middle. Fifty may be the new thirty, but, at the same time, has twelve become the new twenty-five?

Of course many mothers believe that dressing up and make-up is just child's play. And it is – up to a point. For some parents, giving their daughter a Barbie-doll childhood is an innocent way of rejoicing in and celebrating the fact that they have a girl. They are reliving their own youth and still remember the delight of painting their nails for the first time.

But when the demand for the beautification of children becomes so great that children's spas and makeover parties start to become mainstream, we need to ask what messages we are sending our girls. However innocently we intend it, by dressing our daughters to look older than their age, we risk them behaving in ways they aren't emotionally mature enough to handle. Most dangerously of all, we also let them believe that how they look is the most valuable thing about them. As our girls' first role models, we need to start setting some boundaries again. I hear many mothers account for the fact that their little girls have pierced ears, dress in sexy outfits, or plaster themselves with make-up with the words: "Once she gets the idea, there's no stopping her." But it's too early to let children be in charge – and the people who should be stopping them are their parents.

We also need to ask some searching, and painful, questions about where our girls are getting the idea that they need to be waxed, preened, and primped. Is it from the media, or from us – or a self-reinforcing combination of both? As we became women ourselves, in the first media-saturated, appearance-obsessed age, the growing pressure on all women to look better and be slimmer was gradually insinuated by the proliferation of magazines, TV shows, and movies. We have to take great care not to offload our own insecurities onto our daughters, and break the cycle before it gets reinforced again. Otherwise the young girls who innocently observe us fretting all the time about how we look will assume that's just what women do.

We need to mentor our children, but not as if we were coaching them to win a beauty contest. Mothers should provide the down-to-earth perspective girls need when they get buffeted by comparisons, competition, faltering confidence, and classroom spitefulness. We should not be the people putting them on the catwalk of life in the first place. It's impossible to know in what ways your daughter will want to be like you and in what ways she won't. By all means pass on what you have learned and share your experiences, but resist imposing your ambitions, insecurities, and expectations about looks on her too.

Parenting is also as much about what you don't say as what you do say. There is a difference between being honest and open with your child and blurting out your insecurities for your benefit, not hers. Sometimes, when we are caught off-guard, it can take an almost superhuman act of self-control not to complain that we look dreadful or feel as though we've gained a few pounds – as if it was the end of the world. Your daughter is not your confidante, she is your child. She is not your best friend, she is your ultimate responsibility. So stay conscious of the words you say and the messages you send. Make yours a connection based on all the wonderful things you can share with her – not whether you get your nails and highlights done together.

"Everything looks good on her"

"Everything looks good on her. I'm jealous," said Madonna as she let her thirteen-year-old daughter, Lourdes, launch her own raunchy fashion line in front of the world's press. It's a feeling that many of us have to face up to as we get older and pass the baton of youthful sexuality to our daughters. At the same time as I have heard mothers complain that they can't hold back prematurely sexualizing influences on their daughters, I have also seen them enviously admire their daughters' slender, cellulite-free limbs, on display under micro miniskirts. As grown-up women, we have to be careful that we don't unconsciously allow our growing girls to dress the way we might like to dress if our bodies were thirty years younger. Look hard at where you end and your daughter begins.

What fathers can do

"My dad was always making remarks about what women looked like. He rated everyone like a prize heifer and mainly seemed to value my mum because she was pretty. As I grew up, I found myself judging myself on that basis too. It made me feel I was never pretty enough for any man."
Tessa, 42

"My husband can't understand why this adoring little girl has turned into this surly teenager. So he keeps away while I act as the go-between and sometimes dry the tears."
Toni, 44

"I was incredibly close to my dad growing up. I just felt so loved and accepted – and he and my mum made such a great team. He was the first man who loved me – and he may be a tough act to follow, but I know I am worth it."
Laura, 21

If you are a father reading this, you are the first man in your daughter's life – and that is a huge responsibility. While she will look to her mother to learn how to be a woman, she will look to you for male approval. In an era when girls are encouraged by society to please men with the way they look and act, giving her the security of your unconditional love can be a very powerful protection.

Of course, you may feel that just by providing material security, and being "around" as a stable role model, you're doing enough. But in fact your daughter needs you more than that – and a father's semi-present aloofness can be even more hurtful and confusing. To a little girl, being in the same room as a father who is parked behind a laptop or a newspaper can feel like a double betrayal – you are present, for once, but you still pay her no attention. Because of the way girls tend to blame themselves first, they tend to think it's *their* fault you don't spend time with them, not that you are busy.

Of course, it's harder when the perky, eager-to-please daddy's girl turns into a sullen teenager. But at this point it's even more important that fathers don't back off. Resist the temptation to withdraw. Having a father who is involved during the stormy time of puberty makes a huge difference to how a girl feels about herself. In fact, overall, researchers believe that her father may have even more of a role in building a girl's self-esteem than her mother. While, rightly or wrongly, a girl sees it as her mother's natural role to care for her, she feels that time spent with her dad is *his* choice.

If you give her the reassurance that you love the person she is becoming, she will face the world more confidently, knowing she can be herself. The effects of a father's unconditional love are lifelong. According to the Children's Society, daughters of men who are more closely involved develop better friendships, more empathy, and higher self-worth, and are happier with their lives. A father's involvement in a girl's life, as early as toddlerhood, predicts both a girl's self-esteem and her achievements at secondary school. If girls are close to their fathers they are also less likely to have sex at an early age.[17] On the other hand, researchers have found that girls who are in conflict with their fathers tend to be more aggressive, more bullying, and more likely to get into trouble.

It may be hard, but just as mothers have to examine their own attitudes to body image and dieting, fathers may also have to question their own attitudes to the opposite sex. Do you value all your daughter's strengths equally? Do you actually listen to her opinion? Or do you sometimes trivialize her because she's a girl? When it comes to your partner, do you treat her as an equal? Or have you started to lump her and your daughter together as a mysterious, alien species – women – which you will never understand? If you do pay your daughter compliments, do you find yourself more often congratulating her for being obedient and "good" than your son? Crucially, do you ever judge your daughter by what she looks like? Do you affectionately or approvingly refer to her as a heart-breaker or a "little cracker", or joke that you'll need to fight the boys off when she's older?

If so, be aware of how your daughter could turn those messages back on herself. A University of Auckland survey of more than 200 daughters of men who placed great importance on a woman's appearance found that they were much more likely to have made themselves sick to lose weight. Every single one of these girls believed she was fatter than she should be.[18] More dangerously, if you turn away from your daughter, she may start to wonder how she needs to change, what she needs to do differently, to get you to notice her. As parenting educators Ian and Mary Grant observe in their book *Raising Confident Girls*, some of the most rebellious teenage girls became that way when their fathers took a hands-off approach in their adolescent years. "It's as if the girls had something inside them that made them test their fathers to see if they would fight for them."[19]

When helping your daughter grow up, don't feel disadvantaged just because you've never been a girl growing up yourself. The fact that you are less likely to be caught up in the sometimes fractious relationships between mothers and daughters means you can help keep the ship steady. Your point of view is also invaluable because you can decode how males think for her. Don't fall into the trap of telling her: "They're only after one thing." Assure her there will be good men out there who will value her – and she should reserve the right to choose carefully.

Above all, make your love unconditional. Men tend to be more target-driven than women, but don't think that your role is to set goals for your daughter. When your five-year-old learns to swim a width, resist the temptation immediately to urge her to try a length. To a girl, elated by her new achievement, this sounds like a criticism that she hasn't done enough. Celebrate her efforts, not just the end result. Love her for who she is, not just for how good she looks – or makes you look. Without being overly protective, let her know you are always there for her. By treating her with dignity and respect, set the standard for male behaviour that she will expect other men to follow. By giving your acceptance, you can save her needing to prove her worth to men, because she knows how valuable and lovely she is to you.

What you can do:

Start early. Fathers often feel excluded by the mother–daughter relationship. When a baby cries for its mother first, some men feel rejected and quickly retreat into the belief that a girl only needs her mum. From an early age, get involved and stay involved.

Work around your daughter. In these days when more of us are able to work from home with more flexible hours, look at ways you could be more involved in your girl's day-to-day life. If you work full-time out of the home, look for ways to prioritize time with her. She won't be a child for long.

Find things you can do together. Set aside – and stick to – a special, regular, uninterrupted time for you and your daughter to spend together. Let her decide what you do together so she feels she has some control in your relationship.

Don't judge other women by their looks in front of your daughter. Never denigrate any female on the basis of looks – and especially not of weight – as your daughter may think that men will judge *her* on that basis.

Keep hugging. Fathers may feel less comfortable about cuddling their girls as they get older. But keep showing your affection physically – even if it's just a squeeze or a stroke of the hand.

Be fair. If you also have sons, invite both girls and boys to do the same activities to teach your daughters they have equal abilities.

Don't make her into your little girl in need of protection. It makes dads feel fatherly and macho to pretend that their daughters are delicate flowers. But feeling competent is a major pillar of self-esteem, so don't take it away from her by making her feel incapable. Encourage her to feel she can do anything, by teaching her traditionally male skills, such as DIY skills.

Ask her mum to be a go-between. If you're unsure what's happening with your daughter, ask her mother for some translation, rather than asking your daughter outright or blundering into things. Your daughter may well be sensitive about her growing body in ways you are not aware of. Never tease her about her appearance. She may laugh along, but girls are so sensitive that even the most gentle mickey-taking and nicknames are never forgotten – and may not be forgiven.

Building an extended family

As much as we try to be everything to our children, it helps to have other people around who also have their best interests at heart. When your views inevitably start to carry less sway with your daughter in her teenage years, the presence of other responsible adults who share your values – and whom your daughter respects – can have a steadying effect, especially when your input isn't always appreciated. Nurture relationships with aunts, grandparents, family friends, and trusted neighbours who will be there for her if she wants to talk about subjects she can't address with you. Introduce her to strong, independent women in your family whom she can respect and model herself on.

Don't let the only contact you have with your child's godparents be presents through the post at Christmas and birthdays, as so often happens with the passing years. Involve them in your lives, so they can live up to their commitment to guide her. Set up dates in the diary when they can actively get to know her better. It can be a big boost to a child's self-esteem to know that there are other grown-ups who want to spend time with her.

Although it is harder after the primary school years, still make an active effort to get to know the mothers of your daughter's friends. As she gets older and spends more time at their houses, it will help to know that there are other adults looking out for her, who hopefully have similar concerns. Ultimately your daughter will feel safer in the knowledge that there is a support network of grown-ups around her who love and care for her.

What schools can do

Even though several progressive head teachers have stood up to talk about the challenges facing our daughters today, generally schools tend to leave the issue of early sexualization in the hands of parents. That's a shame because, while it's true that parents bear the first responsibility, it's a far bigger challenge than can be handled by families alone. Not only can schools help to support parents' values, they can also assist parents as a group in being more mindful; and by introducing school rules on issues such as mobile phones, make-up, and Facebook, they can help families act collectively against unhelpful influences.

Some schools are prepared to take a stand – such as St Aidan's Church of England school in Yorkshire, which has told girls to start wearing trousers because they were wearing their skirts too short. But others turn a blind eye to the sexist messages that can pervade school life if left unchecked.

When it comes to the sensitive feelings of teenagers, teachers need to tread carefully. One fourteen-year-old I spoke to experienced a serious blow to her self-esteem when teachers organized a joke end-of-year prize-giving. She had been voted "Girl most likely to wear the most make-up". To be a good sport, she pretended to take it with good grace – even though the reason she wore foundation was because of her spots. Privately, she was devastated.

Parents may also question the advisability of heads arranging US-style "proms", sometimes for children as young as seven. This may amuse adults, but at such a young age many girls and boys feel mortified by the pressure to "choose a date" when they don't yet have any interest in forming proto-romantic relationships. As Diane Levin suggests in her book *So Sexy, So Soon*, the best way for schools and parents to work together is by creating an atmosphere in which teachers and parents co-operate, share information, and help each other in limiting children's exposure to harmful influences. She says: "When this happens, it's a win-win situation for everyone but the marketers."[20]

What you can do:

Question the need for school dances and proms before children are ready. If schools want to encourage primary school boys and girls to mix better, ask them to think of hobby activities such as movie clubs, hiking, or sports rather than events that force children to feel they should be thinking about each other romantically. If the school insists on putting on discos, encourage children to believe they don't have to go in boy–girl couples and it's fine to go in groups of friends.

Ask schools to be mindful of the messages they send out. Despite the amount of attention paid to sexualization, there are still plenty of inappropriate messages being passed around via jokes, satirical magazines, and suggestive musical numbers in dance clubs and school discos. Without wishing to sound too PC, suggest that some schools could be more thoughtful. Don't apologize or go silent if something slips through the net. You don't have to be strident or difficult, or embarrass your child. But in order to protect your daughter, you need a voice too. Other parents or the head teacher don't have to agree with the points you raise, but at least your objections will get them thinking.

Make self-esteem a priority for your child's teacher. If you feel your child has low self-esteem then talk to her teachers so they are aware of your worries. Quiet, under-confident children are often allowed to fade into the background. Then, when your daughter is never picked for a team, it confirms her poor opinion of herself. Ask teachers to help you find ways of breaking this cycle – and choose a school for your child which makes building self-esteem a top priority.

"Just the way you are": loving our girls unconditionally

At the other end of the Childline phone line, sixteen-year-old Alice is inconsolable. Through her sobs, she tells the counsellor that she's in the middle of taking her A-levels, and she's been predicted all top grades. But, over and over again, she repeats that she won't be able to get the results and she's going to let her parents down. Her mother and father know nothing about how she feels. More than that, she feels guilty because they are paying for her to have coaching.

We start off trying to build the perfect world for our girls. But then they end up thinking they have to be perfect too. There are league tables to compete in and expectations to live up to. They have to look good, be in the popular clique, be a certain size, and look a certain way. Girls suffer much more than boys because, particularly as young children, they tend to try to be "good girls".

Now that girls are outperforming boys at school and they have similar opportunities in the workplace, many loving parents tend to set the highest goals for their daughters. But while some girls will rise to the challenge, others, who are pushed too far, will cave in under the pressure. Even though it's not always obvious in the teenage years, the fear of letting their parents down is a huge influence on girls' behaviour. If we take advantage of that natural conscientiousness and turn girls into extensions of our own ambitions, or use them to settle our own outstanding scores in life, then this can become an unbearable load to carry at a critical time.

From early on, your child needs to know that she can't be good at everything. No one can be. The risk is that girls who feel like losers academically may just give up and find other ways to assert their individuality in our sexualized society. On top of striving to get good marks, girls also try to live up to the images of physical perfection that the media set them. Most will fail, and will end up blaming themselves for not being good enough.

That's why it's so important not to attach conditions or expectations to your love for your daughter. You probably tell her you love her several times a day. Indeed, although it's always nice to hear, she probably expects you to say it. After all, you are her parent. You may say it so many times it sounds like a reflex. But by adding the phrase "just the way you are" you will give your daughter a feeling of acceptance which she will find deeply reassuring, and you will help her to accept herself. Far from breeding complacency, these five words have the power to convince her that you are completely on her side, which is what she needs most.

Just saying you love them unconditionally is the easy part. In reality, it's much harder to put into practice than it sounds. If, deep down, you want your child to be something else – more academic, more sporty, thinner, or more outgoing – ask yourself why. What is it about *you* that makes you need these things? Check that you aren't giving and withholding affection according to how your daughter performs. Do you feel more warmly towards her when she does well at school? Is your love for her influenced by how good she is making you look as a parent?

Girls always pick up these signals, loud and clear. And if she thinks nothing she does is ever going to be enough, she may give up trying. If she feels she is not being listened to, she may try and find another means of expressing herself – perhaps through eating disorders, self-harm, or promiscuity – and it will be a voice you won't want to hear.

What you can do:

Check your competitive urges. If by the age of eight or nine your daughter starts feeling blamed and acts defensively, it may be a clue that you are attaching too many conditions to your affection. Equally if you can't set eyes on your daughter without feeling the urge to comment or question, then maybe it's time to become more relaxed in your parenting style.

Don't burden her with your expectations. Just because you were top of the class at English doesn't mean she has to be. You may have to delve deep to find out why you place pressure on your daughter to succeed. Be fair to her by being realistic about what she can achieve.

Don't expect her to do well all the time. When children are praised for being clever, it doesn't necessarily make them feel happy and satisfied with themselves. Instead the need to maintain this image becomes a prime concern, especially among the most academic children. Girls especially can become convinced they are not allowed to fail – and become stressed. So tell your daughter you expect her to fail sometimes, and that sometimes failure can be the best lesson of all.

Allow her to take risks. As parents, our instinct is always to try to catch our daughters before they fall. But over-protectiveness does not serve them well. It may sound clichéd, but arm girls with a few phrases such as "We miss 100 per cent of the shots we never take".

Don't make winning the only goal. Break every task into small, achievable steps in the right direction. Praise the effort, not the achievement.

PART 2

How self-esteem and communication are your daughter's best defence

Take a browse through the Facebook pages of older tweens and teenage girls, and they look confident, even brazen. They pout, parade, and show off for the camera. But scratch the surface and you may find this is not real confidence, but bravado borrowed from pop videos and celebrity gossip culture. In fact, statistics on depression, anxiety, and self-harm show our girls are more unsure than ever before – and their fragile sense of self is too often based on where they come in the classroom beauty contest, how hot boys think they are, and how popular they are.

After all, from every direction, our girls are being inundated with messages that they have to be thinner, prettier, cleverer, sexier, richer, and better dressed. Advertisers, the internet, magazines, the fashion industry, and television get children hooked by telling them they are simply not good enough, attractive enough, or cool enough. Of course the ultimate goal for parents should be a society in which those messages are switched off. But that's still a long way away and, until it arrives, we need to protect our daughters by helping them develop a strong sense of self-acceptance. Giving your daughter a secure identity will help to immunize her against any need she may feel in her teenage years to win approval from her peers through precocious sexual behaviour, and against the insecurities that might lead her to feel she has to conform to the "so sexy" stereotype.

Although she may be hurt by the inevitable put-downs that everyone experiences, they won't shake her inner self because, ultimately, she will know herself better than that. Overall, if she has strong self-esteem, she will feel she is likeable and won't rely on friends who may encourage her to act against her true self. She will tend to feel in control and make better choices because she knows, likes, and trusts herself. She will be happier being an individual who makes her own judgments and decisions.

There are a lot of parenting books out there, on subjects ranging from how to be a fabulous mum to how to make your child brilliant. There are entire shelves devoted to the skills you need to get children into routines, deal with toddler tantrums, and handle potty training. But beyond that, there is not so much available on the single most important way to ensure the happiness and emotional safety of your child: building in her a realistic sense of self-acceptance and self-worth.

Of course, all parents set out with the vague and general aim of *wanting* their daughters to feel good about themselves. But it's a question of how high a priority we give this goal, alongside our needs to see our children get good exam results, look good – and reflect well on us. I hear a lot of parents rush to say how "bright" their children are, patting themselves on the back about how they have a string of A-star GCSEs, good A-levels, and university offers. But while parents speak glowingly of their daughter's "confidence", I rarely hear them extolling what's more important: a healthy sense of self-esteem. Because with all the good looks, popularity, and exam success in the world, our girls will never be truly happy or successful without it.

That's why developing self-esteem in our daughters should be the first and most important goal, not something that we hope they pick up along the way. Parents may be reluctant to make self-esteem a priority because it gets confused with vanity or arrogance. But there are important differences between an inflated self-regard, based on empty praise, self-centredness, and the need to show off, and a solid sense of self-worth, based on reality.

Here are just some of the benefits your daughter will reap from a strong identity – and every single one will also protect her from the effects of early sexualization.

- She won't desperately need the approval of her peer group for everything she does or wears.
- She will know herself well enough to be able to brush off and fight back against bitchy put-downs. If she's bullied, she will know it's not her fault.
- She won't seek out sex to make her feel desirable, or worthwhile.
- She won't believe she is defined by what she owns or wears.
- She will choose partners who are worthy of her, and be drawn to healthy relationships over unhealthy ones.
- She will take good risks because she has the belief and trust in herself to find out what she is truly capable of.
- She will forgive herself for failure and get back up again.

Self-esteem: the best safeguard

As soon as she is born, your daughter's self-image starts off being almost entirely dependent on what you, her parents, say and how you respond to her. When, as a toddler, your child tells you: "I'm a good girl," it's because she's been told so by you and by the other adults raising her.

But after the simplicity of those early years, promoting self-esteem is about much more than just *telling* our daughters we love them. That's the easy part. Self-esteem in children also comes from feeling competent, capable, and connected to a larger world. As your daughter gets older, it's derived from knowing herself, and appreciating what she's already achieved and how she has made a difference.

Of course, your daughter's opinion of herself fluctuates all the time. From day to day, from hour to hour, our girls are in a constant conversation with themselves, in which they question their abilities and attributes. Your nine-year-old may feel great about herself the day she scores a goal in a netball match, but terrible about herself the day her best friend decides she wants to spend break-time with someone else.

We parents can help our girls develop the resilience they need to handle the ups and downs of life. We can help them learn that if they fall down, they can get up again. It won't stop your daughter from failing, but it might give her a safety net when she does. By helping our girls to view their strengths realistically and learn new skills, and by showing them that they are loved for who they are, not what they do, gradually we can help them to develop an inner core enabling them to stand firmer against the negative influences around them.

What you can do:

Tell your daughter how lucky you are to have her. Say how privileged you feel to help raise her. Tell her all the ways she has changed your life for the better.

See the whole child. Sometimes parents can slip into the habit of summing up their daughter based on a few characteristics that either bother or please them the most: "She's very pretty, but she's rather dreamy", or, "My daughter is competitive and sporty." Don't label, or your daughter will absorb these tags into her sense of identity. Give her the freedom to be who she wants to be.

Don't generalize or exaggerate bad points. Never tell your daughter she *always* does anything, because then she will be unable to escape your typecasting.

Tell her she is unique. If you tell your daughter there is only one person in the world like her, you will be telling her the truth. Don't compare her – for good or bad – with anyone else.

Tell her you like her. Most children expect us to love them. We're their parents – it's our job. But liking is a choice. When we tell our daughter we like her, we are saying we like spending time with her and the person she has become.

Help her feel connected to others. Making your daughter feel important in the bigger picture will also help build lasting self-esteem. Encourage her to join a choir, orchestra, youth or campaign group so she feels a vital part of the wider world.

Find a sport she likes. Keep searching until she finds one she likes and which suits her personality and physique. Make physical activity a fun part of who you are as a family, whether it's playing tag or going cycling in the park. Sport gives girls co-ordination, body confidence, and leadership skills. Strength is also a powerful protection – both psychologically and physically. Girls who take self-defence classes generally feel more safe and confident in the world. Furthermore, when your child learns what her body can do, as well as how it looks, she is less likely to criticize its appearance.[21]

A word on praise

"Amazing, darling!"; "Good effort!"; "Well done!". Words of praise like these become so common they're like a reflex action. Indeed at some school events, it almost sounds like a competitive sport as to which parent can lavish their child with the most superlatives. Many parents believe they are giving their girls self-esteem by constantly telling them how well they are doing at everything from eating their breakfast in the morning to going to bed at night. The problem is that after a while your daughter has heard "Well done" so many times that the words become meaningless.

As girls get older and go out into the real world, they soon realize that not everything they do is "amazing", or "brilliant" for that matter, and that you're just saying it because you're their parent. They stop believing your assessment of them, and their faith in your judgment – which they need to trust – is diminished.

A better way to make your daughter feel good about her achievements is to show that you really notice what she does, rather than love-bombing her with vague, catch-all praise. First of all, simply acknowledge what she is doing right. Take time to stop and notice it. Tell her: "You've put all your clothes away," or, "You've done your homework without being asked." Then tell her what's right about it: "Tomorrow you'll know where to find everything," or, "Now I won't have to remind you about it any more." By complimenting her on the fine details of what she's done right, instead of criticizing her for doing wrong, you will show your daughter that you are truly paying attention – and she will want to do it again.

What you can do:

Use your mind – and your body – to give praise. Make sure you maintain eye contact to show you really mean what you say, and follow it up with a hug, pat on the back, wink, or squeeze of the hand.

Don't undermine your praise. You may think you are just egging your children to do even better, but qualifying your congratulations with an encouragement to do even more can be deeply demoralizing. Acknowledge and appreciate their achievements – and leave it there.

Let her reward herself. Praise should come from the inside as well as the outside. Teach girls that they are also entitled to reward themselves for something they are proud of – whether it's with a bubble bath when they've had a tough day or a favourite film.

Don't over-praise. Bigging up your daughter more than she deserves actually ends up short-circuiting self-esteem. The danger is that your daughter will build her self-image on a fantasy of superiority that will inevitably come crashing down. Or, if she is a more sensitive child, she could grow to become embarrassed or reluctant to accept compliments, even when they are due, because she feels they are not justified and she has lost faith in your judgment. Acknowledge and appreciate her successes – but keep it in proportion.

Don't praise by comparison. Against our better judgment, it can be tempting to think we are boosting our child's self-esteem by coming out with things like: "You're the prettiest girl in the class," or, "I bet your story was the best one." But this kind of one-upmanship not only encourages children to repeat the sentiments – making them unpopular with their peers – it also teaches girls that they are only valued by how well they do compared with others. Instead, let her achievements stand in their own right, and encourage her to measure herself against her own personal best, not other children's.

How to teach your daughter to feel good about herself: building confidence from within

Have you ever seen the huge and natural smile on your child's face when she has done something for the first time – all by herself? Every time your child feels that sensation, it's another building block in her self-esteem. Self-esteem does not just come from our telling our children they are capable and clever, although praise certainly helps if it's sincere and targeted. Children need to feel self-worth from within themselves too.

But it's ironic that while our girls are growing up faster than ever in the virtual world, we allow them less and less to prove what they are capable of in the real world. In a climate of fear, intensified by round-the-clock television news and alarm over paedophiles, it's very tempting to overprotect our daughters in everything they do. But while we may think we are safeguarding them from injury and physical harm, really we are also denying our children the chance to feel good, explore nature, climb trees, and learn to look after themselves. One in ten parents doesn't let their children play outside because it's dirty, according to a survey by the Children's Society. One in five seven- to fourteen-year-olds plays outside for less than an hour a week. Yet nearly two in five children complain they don't play outdoors as much as they would like.[22] By condemning our girls to a "battery hen" existence and allowing them to spend all their time with computers, just so we know where we can find them, they enter a world of cyber dangers where the threats are different, but in their own ways just as great.

If we deny our children independence and responsibility it is taken by them to mean we have no confidence in their abilities. While you may hope that cosseting them makes them feel safe and cared for, in fact they feel helpless. Because childhood is a process of learning to do new things, children believe you are waiting on them hand and foot because they are incapable. Ultimately this also undermines your authority – and you will need every ounce of that in the years to come. As the parenting educator Noel Janis-Norton points out: "Children don't respect servants." Check that your fears about your daughter's safety and well-being are in proportion to reality. Ask yourself who you are really protecting here. Is it them – or are you doing it for your own peace of mind? So whether it's making an omelette or changing a light-bulb, think first about what your daughter is ready to do for herself – not what you can do for her.

Choosing parenting priorities: being there and making time

Once again, let's go back to the beginning. From the moment we held our first baby girl in our arms, we promised we would try to be the perfect parent. We vowed to read the right parenting books, say the right things, and spend all our time playing with and caring for this delightful little creature. So the first part of building our daughter's self-esteem should have been blissfully easy. When she cried and we responded by picking her up, we taught her the first lesson in feeling good about herself – that she is a valued person who deserves to be heard.

As our babies grew into toddlers, we continued to work hard to protect and cherish our girls. We cuddled them, played with them, and usually followed the childcare manuals to the letter. But somewhere along the way, other pressures, such as work and the need to earn money, started to steal away the hours we meant to spend with our little girl. Gradually, day by day, then year by year, many of us became less and less the mothers and fathers we set out to be.

Over time, did the time you once devoted to sitting down and playing with your daughter dwindle? And, gradually, did you start to see the fact that your children were settled and playing quietly as an opportunity to grab ten minutes to catch up on emails? Many of us have become so stressed that we have fallen for the lure of "anything-for-a-quiet-life" parenting: it's easier to fob children off with computers and video games than interact with them.

But don't make the mistake of thinking your children don't notice when your eyes flick down to your latest text, just because it's become normal – or because they've given up complaining. I'm not saying that we should make our children the centre of the universe every moment of the day. That would breed an unrealistic narcissism. They have to learn where they fit into our lives. But if we only half listen – and allow all our time to become enveloped by the creeping tendrils of technology – we risk losing our essential bond with our girls. Of course, you can tell your daughter you love her a dozen times a day. But if you are texting and looking up at the clock as you do it, the message will be undermined. And what would you do if someone was usually looking the other way when you talked to them? You'd give up.

Sometimes we just need reminding that time is running out. Our girls' childhoods are short. From birth to the age of twelve, we have just 4,380 days with them. Yet sometimes we are so busy trying to give our girls everything materially, we don't give them what they want most – us. This is a corrosive tendency and can create a separation that is hard to heal. If we spend these crucial years checking emails, is it any surprise that our daughters stop looking up from Facebook when we enter the room by the time they are teenagers?

It's a catch-22 on so many levels. The less time you spend with your children, the less interesting you will find them – and the more your eyes will flick back to the latest incoming message. Of course, as loving parents who want everything for our children, an excessively busy lifestyle is not necessarily something we choose. It's something we drift into and then find hard to escape. The demands of the mortgage, the cost of living, and longer working hours that no longer know any limits – because our offices go with us everywhere we go – mean that parenting can become something we squeeze in around our careers.

We get by with the promise that things will get better soon. But as Rob Parsons of Care for the Family points out: "A slower day is not coming."[23] While it's true that you won't ever have more time, what you can do is prioritize the time you do have. You can pay less attention to the things that don't really matter – such as celebrity culture and television – and spend more time on the things that really do – such as your children. Holding ordinary conversations, playing games, doing simple things – cooking or going for walks – with your daughter is all you need to do.

But the time for these things has to be set aside and protected nonetheless. Otherwise, the longer our daughters are left to surf the web, the more likely they are to come across unsuitable internet sites or drift into potentially harmful activities we can't monitor. The less attention they get in the home, the more they may seek outside it.

Your values: how to define them, share them, and agree boundaries

So what exactly are our priorities for our girls? Is it letting them keep up with their friends – or keeping them safe at any cost? For example, do you believe that consensual sex is OK without love? Is it all right for your daughter to go on Facebook before the legal age of thirteen because some of her mates do?

Considering how much time we spend worrying about feeding, clothing, and schooling our children, it's ironic how little we spend thinking about the main messages we want to pass on to them. While we may fret about E-numbers and school league tables, how much thought do we give to the values we want our girls to inherit? One of the reasons parents have been left drowning in the backwash of early sexualization is that we may never have sat down and taken the time to decide what those values are. In the increasingly live-and-let-live secular society that has flourished in the last thirty years, it's been left up to us to decide on our values. But most often, we've ended up not deciding on anything much at all.

Instead we fire-fight when rows flare up. But by the time the dilemma has surfaced, the whole situation is fraught and often whipped into a frenzy by peer pressure.

Whatever you decide, you will be in a much better position if you know where you stand. If you do, there's a better chance that you will be able to maintain consistent messages on which you and your partner can base your joint decisions. But all of this could do more harm than good if you don't stick to the values you've decided on. When our words contradict our actions, our children take the most note of what we do, not what we say. If words and actions conflict, they lose respect for both.

Your values and other people

Once you've decided what your values are, be confident enough to be clear about them to friends, family, teachers, and other parents. When it comes to your daughter, uphold your right to ask others to support the way you want to bring her up, especially if you feel they are encouraging her to grow up faster than you would wish. It may be that other parents around you have not thought about the issues as deeply as you have, and explaining your own reasons for wanting to protect your children may help them consider the implications.

For example, if you've worked hard to avoid your eight-year-old thinking she needs make-up to look pretty and she's invited to a party where make-up is encouraged, say: "Thanks – but not for my child." After all, why, after your careful consideration, would you let another parent undermine your concern for what's healthiest for your child, and start planting the idea in her mind that she needs make-up before she is ready. Pandora's box only needs to be opened once.

As your daughter grows, dilemmas like this will be unavoidable. I know it's hard. My own daughters have friends who invite them to parties where they are encouraged to wear make-up, and who have Facebook pages even though they are under the the legal age of thirteen. But if you explain early on that different families have different values and priorities, and why you believe that certain things are not a good idea, your children are likely to accept it, and you will have safeguarded a little bit more of their childhood.

Past a certain age, your daughter will make her own mind up – and you won't be there when she is making her most difficult choices. But if she knows and understands your values, which have been in place for as long as she can remember, and she understands there's a good reason for them, there's a better chance she will hear your voice in her head as she makes those choices.

What you can do:

Take responsibility for what she sees. Remember that, in the same way that you decide on what fills your child's tummy, you are the one who decides, at least in her early years, what fills her head. Use this time to direct her away from commercialized and sexualized messages you are not comfortable with.

Learn more about parenting. Head teachers have told me that while classes about how to improve children's academic progress are very popular, those on how to improve parenting skills are considerably less so. But, as parents, we can quickly become trapped in negative patterns and ideas. Parenting courses can start you and your partner thinking more deeply about the messages you are giving your children, and help you agree on a way forward. Otherwise you could end up veering between contradictory styles, which is confusing for your child.

Get on the same page. Be consistent with your partner – and keep talking. If you are seriously at odds over parenting values, your daughter will dismiss you both and decide that neither of you knows what you are talking about. Find a middle way you can both agree on for the sake of your daughter.

Discuss your own beliefs. Talk to your daughter about your values and what motivates your decisions in life. Let her see you treat other people with respect and value them for who they are. Explain why you support certain causes.

Talk through scenarios. Pay attention to newspaper stories about the issues facing young girls today – whether they should have access to the morning-after pill, for example – and discuss with your partner how you would feel if you were affected. There's no way to foresee every difficulty, but find out more about your own beliefs by discussing hypothetical situations. As your daughter gets older, ask her what she thinks too, so she knows there are many sides to an issue – as well as where you stand, and why.

Creating boundaries

Once you know your own values, you are ready to decide on your boundaries. It may sound contradictory, but giving children rules is what allows them the freedom to become independent, strong people. Consistency is the best way to help your daughter feel accepted for who she is. She will be safer being herself without having to follow the herd. To a girl trying to find her way, the world actually feels like a safer place when warm, familiar rules are set up for her. Later on she will be less likely to feel the need to assert her individuality through wayward sexual behaviour – or falling in with harmful peer pressure.

But, as helpful as it is to decide on your boundaries, make sure you and your partner are on the same page and coherent: the words "because I say so" won't do. As she grows older, your daughter needs to know that a rule, such as a curfew, arises out of love and concern for her well-being, as well as mature adult judgment, consideration, and experience – not out of your desire to control her, win an argument, or keep her as a child for as long as possible. That way, she is far more likely to respect it.

Experienced mothers have told me that, once the turbulent years had passed, their daughters thanked them for maintaining boundaries. After all, it's the girls who've just come through adolescence who know better than anyone the risks that are out there.

What you can do:

Tell her why the rules are there. Show your daughter that boundaries are not there just because you have the power to impose them, but to keep her safe.

Give her some input. Of course, it is parents who ultimately draw up the rules. But rather than arbitrarily imposing them, ask your daughter some questions about what she thinks they should be. If your values have rubbed off on her, you may be pleasantly surprised by the common-sense answers. If she thinks hard about the rules, rather than having them foisted on her, they will make more sense to her.

Ask her to think about what is appropriate for her age. Ask her why she thinks legal age limits are in place. Discuss with her the legal ages for drinking, smoking, sex, and viewing certain images, so she sees that they apply to the whole of society, not just to her.

Pretending the world is perfect

Of course, it would be wonderful if we could make the world perfect for our daughters. But despite our best efforts, it's never going to be – and we need to prepare them for this undeniable truth. Bringing them up with a fairytale version of life – complete with a handsome prince who will sweep them off their feet – will only set them up for a life in which they will inevitably feel as if they have failed. Be fair. Let them know that there will always be good days and bad days. Show them how, if they take responsibility for decisions and are truthful with themselves, generally the good days will outnumber the bad.

Understandably some parents take the view: "Oh, she doesn't need to know that." They may fear that understanding more about how the world works might make children precocious or "knowing". But in reality, that's more likely to happen if your daughter takes on an inappropriately adult persona without understanding the influences that are at work on her.

EQ: how to teach your daughter emotional intelligence

Developing self-esteem is a long journey along a bumpy road of ups and downs. Emotional intelligence – teaching your daughter to know herself, understand her fears and insecurities and take responsibility for her actions – will oil the wheels on that road. Encouraging her to develop emotional intelligence is as important as teaching her reading, writing, or arithmetic. If you foster your child's insight and self-knowledge, she will learn to recognize how she really feels and why – and learn how to manage her emotions.

Help her to know herself by never dismissing her problems – or trying to solve them for her. The more you give your girl the skills to understand herself and to deal with her own issues, the more secure she will feel in a confusing world. Children who are able to talk about their feelings are also able to use their self-awareness to judge their own values – and to stand by them when they are challenged. When faced with risky situations and dilemmas, emotional intelligence will ultimately help your daughter to recognize what is harmful to her – and what is not.

What you can do:

Teach her skills to help her make sense of the world. The world can seem like a big, scary place to a young child. Help her feel confident by teaching her the facts and skills to navigate it from the first – starting with the days of the week and months, basic geography, telling the time, and knowing left from right.

Show her how to name – and respond to – negative feelings. When a girl hears a voice telling her she's not good enough, she often assumes it's right. Help her to learn to recognize when her gremlins are hurting her or holding her back. Show her how to replace negative thoughts with positive ones. For example, if she's telling herself: "You can't do this," show her she can replace that thought with: "This might be tricky, but I can learn." Give the negative voice a name – such as Blue Meanie – so she can recognize it as something outside herself which she can choose to ignore.

Let her solve her own problems. Teach emotional responsibility. Don't allow her to blame you for the fact that she hasn't done her homework yet or can't find anything suitable to wear. By all means listen patiently to what she has to say when she's upset or angry – and summarize it back to her so she knows you've listened and you've understood. But then help her process her emotions by drawing out the issues at the source of the problem. Let her analyse it, and find her own solution.

Tell her upfront about the effects of hormones. Warn her that during puberty hormonal changes may make her feel more emotional, but they are there to help her grow up. Inform her that mood swings can sometimes make it hard to make good choices, so it's a good idea not to rush into big decisions.

Brainstorm how to work out a problem. Don't pretend you have a magic wand that will fix her feelings. Get her thinking about how to approach a dilemma. Get older siblings involved too and make it into a family project to share your experiences and see if you can find a way of dealing with it together.

Teach her to name her feelings. It can help to teach girls how to describe feelings in pictures – sadness as an iceberg, for example – and recognize how their physical sensations affect the body.

Explain how looking after her brain can make her feel happier. Before the thought of dieting even crosses her mind, explain how "brain foods", such as fish and blueberries, can make her feel happier and boost how well she concentrates at school. Further down the line when she becomes weight conscious, this may help her see that dieting will only make her feel miserable.

Ask her why she thinks people act the way they do. People's behaviour and motivations, so often contradictory and hard to fathom for adults, can be even more confusing and scary for girls trying to make sense of the world. Trying to ascribe motivations is always a dangerous game. But if another child has said something to upset her, try helping her to see the context of the situation. If she can see the remarks in perspective, you can make her aware of the complexities of human behaviour – and help her realize that she is not to blame if someone is cruel to her.

Explain your own emotions and reasons. Don't just say: "Because I say so." Help her to manage her feelings by acknowledging both your own and hers. Let her know why you might be feeling angry or sad, so she realizes it's not about something she's done. Children are sensitive and will often assume they are to blame.

Give your daughter a wider perspective on life. Ask her to think about the questions: "Why I am here? What can I do to make the world a better place by being in it?" She doesn't have to find an answer. But if she focuses on something beyond herself, she's less likely to put long-lasting importance on trivial things such as consumerism and looks.

Respect your child's opinions. Don't dismiss your daughter's opinions because she's a child. Contrary to the image of the compliant "good girl", the fact that a child is developing a strong sense of self may be reflected in the way she will start arguing for her point of view. From around the age of seven, children will pride themselves on being logical and fair, so don't shout down their arguments, tiring though it may be to listen. If there's something important that you really don't agree on, work out a solution together.

Treat your daughter as though she is already the best person she can be. This isn't the same as forcing children to fit your expectations. It's about appealing to the best in their nature to be honest, decent human beings. Treat any bad behaviour as a somewhat surprising deviation from her good character.

Ask your child to be kind to herself. From around the age of eight, girls can start to give themselves a very hard time for saying or doing the wrong thing. First tell her not to be so tough on herself – and tell her how you as an adult have also made mistakes. But also help her heal herself if she feels she has done something wrong. Tell her to replay a painful memory in her head, and imagine herself as her own best friend, going up and giving herself a hug. It sounds sickly, but it's a powerful way for her to visualize self-acceptance and self-forgiveness.

Give her permission to love herself. Little girls are told to love their mummies, daddies, siblings, and pets – yet we often forget to give our daughters permission to love themselves too. Tell her that being her own best friend doesn't make her big-headed, it just means she's looking out for herself.

Explain self-respect. Explain that self-respect means thinking well of yourself, not because you're stuck up, but because you know and appreciate yourself deep down. Explain that if she constantly puts herself down, people won't like her more for it. They will take her at her word.

Don't say: "Never mind"

As I chatted to another mother at a play-date one afternoon, she dropped into the conversation that her seven-year-old daughter had been having trouble sleeping, and would then lie awake worrying that she would not wake up for school the next morning. The child, who had now overheard the conversation, joined in and was trying to explain that the chiming of a clock downstairs as she tried to drop off to sleep was making her even more anxious. The child wanted to elaborate, but the mother repeatedly told her – in a tone which made it clear she wanted her to be quiet – "Never mind, darling. It really doesn't matter." The look of bewilderment as the little girl tried to express how she felt and the mother dismissed her feelings was sad to see.

Children need to be allowed to express the things that frighten and concern them, even if they are inconvenient to us as adults. By saying "never mind" we take away the tools our children have to recognize, name, and deal with emotions. If you tell them their emotions don't matter or they've got them wrong, they stop trusting those emotions. One of the reasons why some young people self-injure is that their feelings are dismissed as wrong or unimportant within their families in some way. They learn that certain feelings aren't permitted. Self-harm becomes their way of articulating what is not allowed.

So acknowledge your daughter's emotions, and assume her feelings are real, however trivial you may consider the reasons behind them to be. We can't bully children out of their worries. Listening brings feelings to the surface, where they can be dealt with.

How to help your daughter find out who she is: creating an unshakeable sense of self

For your daughter to resist the forces of sexualization and negative peer pressure, more than anything she needs a strong, unshakeable vision of who she is, where she has come from and what she has achieved. The good news is that it takes an interested parent just a little time to show her how far she has come.

What you can do:

Underline her achievements. Children quickly forget how much they have learned – especially when they feel they still have a long way to go. Keep chronological scrapbooks showing your daughter her drawings, starting from her first scribbles to her latest masterpiece, as well as her letters – from her first giant alphabet to her joined-up writing. Keep the albums separate for each child, and make each one just about them. I have kept a library of albums charting my daughters' lives. Every time we look back through them, we not only have fun, but also reinforce their sense of who they are and how much they've accomplished.

Help her teach little ones. Children positively brim with pride in themselves when they can pass on something they are good at to younger children. Helping smaller kids with anything from reading to music practice takes a child outside herself, and does wonders for her responsibility and maturity.

Teach her family history. Plotting a family tree, looking back at old pictures, and talking about your heritage gives a sense of belonging and continuity that makes children feel grounded and part of something bigger.

Help her to help others. The Children's Society has found that unselfish people are happier than people who are preoccupied with themselves. Start by getting her to sponsor a child or an endangered animal in another country. Let her pledge her pocket money to Age UK or Comic Relief, or give her old toys to the charity shop. Teach her early how good helping others can feel.[24]

Keep family rituals. Mark milestones, so your child knows you are recognizing and welcoming her getting older. Give a child a sense of occasion about her birthday. This isn't the same as lavishing gifts. Let her know how important she is by spending special time with her on that day. For her first birthday as a teenager, take her away on a small break, so you start those years feeling close and so she feels accepted and special.

Learn from your child. Children delight in knowing more than we do, so pay your daughter the ultimate compliment of learning from her. If she's rehearsing a new song for her school play, learn the words and sing along with her. Ask her advice on anything from helping to plan your next holiday to choosing the ripest fruit when shopping.

Write in her books to mark milestones. One of my most treasured possessions is a copy of *Alice's Adventures in Wonderland*, which my father gave me when I was eight. On an afternoon in October 1975, during which he had sat down and helped me learn my Latin homework, he wrote: "From her dad who always loves her – *etiam* she is *superbus*." The inscription still fills me with a feeling of being loved and valued thirty-five years on.

Don't make a virtue of being ordinary. Some parents are perfectly happy if their children "fit in", and for them to be fine, average, and ordinary. But while fitting in is no bad thing, in my experience this is an attitude which can breed insecure adults who then feel they have to work harder to stand out. Children need to feel unique in some way. It's hard to feel good about yourself if you feel you have nothing particularly special to offer.

Help her find something she can seek solace in. Help your daughter find an activity into which she can escape, and which is separate from school and the pressure to compete. It might be a type of music she likes to listen to or an absorbing craft or skill which gives her a chance to withdraw into herself and relax.

Encourage her to join a youth group outside school. Joining an organization such as the Brownies or Guides will encourage her to get outdoors in a safe environment, as well as pick up skills she wouldn't otherwise learn, which will help her feel more competent.

Let her write her book about herself. Around the age of five, your child will start forming her likes and dislikes in lists. Acknowledge that her tastes are important. Let her start to define herself by encouraging her to write a diary, or fill in an "All About Me" book.

Celebrate her artwork. It's now possible to use your children's drawings and pictures to personalize everything from diaries and place-mats to cushions and mugs. Pay your daughter the compliment of using her artwork or images to decorate the things around you.

Why it's important to help your daughter understand how her brain works: helping her to be in control

Human emotion

Considering that emotions, thoughts, and personality are all formed in the brain, we pay remarkably little attention to how this organ works. So teach your daughter some basic biology. Show her how the brain is divided into sections responsible for different kinds of thoughts – and that these work best when they are all working together. Explain that there are also four basic emotions – joy, sadness, anger, and fear – and that feelings are a cocktail of these. Tell her that each one is useful in its own right and it's fine to express all of them, even if the negative ones can feel frightening. Explain that true outbursts of anger are believed to last no longer than twenty seconds, and how the brain makes chemicals when you are angry which flood the whole body and affect heart-rate and breathing. Show her how deep breaths can help bring her body back to normal.

Just a few basic lessons such as these can help children understand themselves and their reactions – and feel more in control.

Human intelligence

British schools have the highest number of exams and assessments in the world. But not everyone can be top of the class – and for many girls in today's competitive society, this can be a blow to their self-esteem. Unless we step in, it doesn't take long for our children to identify themselves as losers if their academic results are not sparkling. Certainly, when I was at school, you were deemed either "brainy" or "thick".

But the work of Robert Sternberg and Howard Gardner has turned that idea on its head by coming up with the theory of "multiple intelligence". They have found that traditional ways of measuring brainpower are much too narrow and don't take into account all the many different types of skills that develop in the brain.[25] So tell your child there are lots and lots of ways to be clever, and recognize the unique combination of strengths she has – including those that aren't necessarily expressed in classwork. To a child who is not top of the class in traditional subjects, the fact that brainpower is now seen to be a unique combination of different strengths can be deeply reassuring. These can include interpersonal intelligence – the ability to read and understand others – and intrapersonal intelligence – the ability to understand yourself.

Talk to your daughter about people you know with perseverance and ability, but not necessarily glowing exam results, who have done well in life, and tell her that the application of perseverance and determination will always take you far. Rather than letting her believe that intelligence is something she can do nothing about, give her back the initiative. If she understands that neural pathways are built by practice and repetition, nothing will seem beyond her. Explain simply how electrical signals make connections between the nerve cells so they form a network. The more the linked cells are used, the stronger the network becomes, forming a memory and eventually a skill. Tell her that all brains are different and work in slightly different ways. Remind her that no one is good at everything – even Einstein had his limitations.

What you can do:

Help her find her learning style. The three main learning styles are visual (seeing and reading), auditory (hearing and speaking), and kinaesthetic (learning through doing). Ask her teacher to test which style works best for her, so you can help her learn more easily.

Give her a bridge to the next level. When you know your daughter is facing a challenge, prepare her. Is your daughter starting netball for the first time, but doesn't seem very confident? Practise some simple catches and throws so it doesn't feel as daunting. Has she got times tables coming up? Buy her a CD so she can get used to the rhythm and pattern. It's not about giving her an advantage over her classmates. It's about helping her feel more prepared and in control.

Find her strengths. If your child isn't a traditional academic high-flyer, then it's especially important to help her find what she's good at to keep her self-esteem strong. Give her the opportunity to try a few things. Don't force it. When she hits on her talent, it will be obvious, because children naturally like the things they are good at. That feeling of competence will carry over into other areas where she is less confident.

Accept help. Having problems in just one area of learning can be hugely debilitating to a child – especially if it is one of the traditional subjects. Yet teachers I have spoken to say that most parents become very defensive when they suggest a more detailed analysis with an educational psychologist. Every child's brain is different, and helping to pinpoint how it works, and where it may need building up, can save everyone a lot of anger, frustration, and wasted effort.

Your daughter's social skills

In the pushy, get-ahead world where we live, girls may feel like failures because they are not leaders. What parent hasn't also felt a twinge to hear that, yet again, their child has been passed over to be form captain or for a part in the school play? But it's important not to see such things as failure. Rather than allowing her to feel she has fallen short, tell her there are many ways of making contributions – behind the scenes too. Show her how to take pride in the less public ways she contributes her unique ideas and personality.

Parents can also get frustrated and embarrassed when their girls are shy. Usually they will get over it as they get older – as long as we don't reinforce it by constantly pointing it out. But along the way, girls can suffer excruciating discomfort in social situations, which can set them back further than they need to be. There's nothing wrong with teaching her a few conversation starters such as: "What music do you like?" or "What's your favourite game?" – and show her how to make brief eye contact when she meets someone new. By doing this, you will be setting up a positive cycle so that people will naturally react more warmly to her, and that will make her feel better about herself.

When your child's self-esteem is suffering through lack of friends

It's not only heartbreaking for a parent to watch her daughter having trouble making friends, but it can be devastating for a girl's self-esteem. Even relatively mild communication problems can have serious effects on feelings of self-worth at a critical age. Children who feel unpopular are more likely to be depressed and get involved in risky behaviour as they get older.

At the age of nine, Victoria is the type of child that the other girls in her class describe as "a bit weird". There's something about her body language and the way she "hovers" at the edge of their games – but doesn't join in – which makes them uncomfortable. From time to time, Victoria also pipes up with "funny" things at unexpected times in lessons – the last time was when she talked about where she went on holiday in Maths class. Behind her back, although never to her face, the other children complain too that Victoria is a "show-off" because she talks "at" them instead of just joining in their conversations.

Whereas traditionally child psychologists focused on school work, more and more they are now looking at the effects of how well children fit in socially. It's always been assumed that this is something that kids do naturally – even if some are better at it than others. Now, for the first time, child specialists are looking at the possibility that not knowing how to make friends is just as much of a learning difficulty as conditions such as dyslexia. They are studying children who are often viewed by other kids as stuck-up, bossy, overbearing, or "geeks".

Child language therapists now believe that a delay in the way a child's brain processes social cues affects how they get on with their peers. Just as dyslexic children can't form words out of the jumble of letters in front of them, children with social learning problems – now known as dyssemia – can't read the right messages from facial expressions and body language. For an ordinary child, it takes an average of three seconds to work out social cues. However, the brain of a child with dyssemia may be slow to read these signals. They have problems working out how other people see them, and difficulties with forming the open body language they need to join in a group, as well as with how to judge when to say the right things at the right time.

Many parents, not knowing what to do, ignore problems of this kind. They may try to explain away their child's behaviour by saying, "Oh, she's just not very good in social situations," or "Grown-ups love her… she's just too grown up for kids her age." But the good news is that the brain is a very malleable organ and the social skills that children need to fit in can be taught. In the same way as children can overcome academic learning disabilities, the child communication expert Michelle Garcia Winner, who is pioneering an approach to the problem called "Social Thinking" in the US, says awkward children can also be taught the social skills they need. "Even if they don't get it by intuition, we can teach children how to be social detectives – to think about how others see them and to use their eyes, ears and brains to learn what is expected from them. Some children just may need more help understanding these concepts than others."[26]

What you can do:

Explain social intelligence. Tell your daughter that, in the same way children can be good at Maths or English, they can also be socially intelligent, and that this can be improved through practice.

Teach her to be a "social detective". Use movies, TV shows, or commercials to give your daughter practice in making guesses about what the on-screen characters will do next based on their facial expressions and body language.

Teach her about body language. Explain how it affects the way other children see her. For example, tell her she will need to turn the front of her body towards a group – and maintain the right distance – to let other kids know she wants to join in a game.

Teach her about eye contact. Explain that if she doesn't use her eyes to look at people, other children will think she is not being friendly. Tell her she needs to "think with her eyes" to work out what are the right social steps to be accepted and included by other children.

If your child can't make friends, seek help. Don't waste time thinking she will grow out of it, because peer exclusion can cause long-term damage to her self-esteem that's difficult to reverse. Find out more at www.socialthinking.com. In Britain, the experts at Calmer, Easier, Happier Parenting in north London also run courses and talks on the subject.[27]

Keeping the conversation going: how to keep the lines of communication open

When your child is being fast-tracked through childhood it's easy to feel overwhelmed and unable to keep up. It can be especially difficult in the teenage years, when your daughter may not appear to care about your opinion, and is much more interested in what her friends have to say. It's fair to say that communication will get very much harder as she gets older. The eight-year-old who won't stop chattering can turn into a morose teenager who's unlikely to offer you more than an eye-roll if you dare to ask how her day has been.

But if you get things right, you can stay close, and be there to protect her. Before your daughter's peers start to drown you out, you will need to build up all the loving respect you can earn and get the channels of communication firmly in place. Stephen R. Covey, author of *The 7 Habits of Highly Effective People* series of books, talks about making "emotional deposits".[28] These are good experiences that help our children know that we love them, and make them more likely to keep listening because they truly know that everything we do is for them. This means that when the difficult times come, as they inevitably will, our girls are more like to hear us out and trust our advice, guidance, and insight.

Especially as your daughter grows more independent, there may well be days when you will find yourself saying no more than a few rushed words in between her coming home from school and you coming home from work. So it's more important than ever that you set aside dedicated time to be with her. And if the rows and sulks leave you dreading the sound of your child's key in the door, then it's definitely time to fix what's gone wrong in your relationship.

At some point she will slam doors, and she will call you every name under the sun. But through it all speak to her – as much as is humanly possible – in the same way as you would want to be spoken to. If you yell, she will simply feel justified in shouting back, and the really important messages won't get through. Try listening again. Is she really trying to push you away, or is she just trying to change the way you communicate by forcing you to recognize she is not a child any more? Most teenage rows are really about her insistence that you should start to acknowledge her as an adult.

Be the grown-up that you are. Ask her to come and chat to you when you are making dinner, running errands, or getting ready to go out. But also set aside times when it's just the two of you, to see how she is, not to nag her about her school work. Take her for coffee or go to a museum together. Make it one-to-one time when she has the chance to say things she might not otherwise have the opportunity to say. But above all, let her know that she always has a voice – even if it's to say things you may not find palatable or easy to deal with.

Remember that girls are natural secret-keepers. Know that just as you probably tell her what you think she needs to know, she may also only be telling you half the story about what she and her friends are up to. For example, she may mention scenarios that happened to "friends" (but never to her, of course) just to see how you react. It may still be hard to get her to open up. Girls are so keen to present a "perfect" image, and do not want to let their parents down. But even if she paints just half the picture, she will feel better and you will be closer than you were. By making it very clear that she is entitled to make mistakes, that you have made some too, and that you won't judge or punish her, you are putting across the important message that she can always come to you.

At a neutral time explain that she will always feel better getting problems off her chest, even if she doesn't look forward to telling you about them. Tell her that you will only be able to help her get to the source of a problem if she's honest with you. You may not know all the answers, but at least you've kept the conversation going, and given her your best perspective on the events in her life, in the hope of helping her to make good judgments. When she talks, just sit there and listen. Like most of us, she probably simply wants to be heard.

What you can do:

FOR YOUNGER GIRLS:
Let her come up with conversation topics. Find out what interests your child and let her talk. Even if you think you know what your daughter will say, just listen and see if you can expand the topic. Try not to interrupt, and give her extra time so she doesn't feel rushed or intimidated.

Go with the phases. Are you secretly ready to scream if you hear the plot of the latest Harry Potter one more time, or the subtle differences between every species of Moshi Monster? Bite your tongue. Know that it's just a phase and most will only last a short time. You will be paying your child the ultimate compliment. Even if you're secretly bored to death, it is more important that she wants to share her interests with you and that you are keeping open the lines of communication.

Share her enthusiasms. Many phases will be more bearable if you take an active interest in what she's talking about. Some of my children's biggest delights have been when I have sat down to play a game they love. If you take part it will become less boring, and they'll feel great that they've interested you in something they discovered.

Look at her when you talk to her. Cup her head in your hands and look into her eyes to show you are really listening.

Keep reading aloud. She may well be able to read to herself by the age of eight, but don't stop there. You are giving your special time, and staying connected. At a time when so much entertainment is digital, reading can also allow her to explore situations and other people's emotional experiences at a more manageable rate, and with your guidance. Help her to find out more about herself by asking about the character's dilemmas and what she would do in their situation.

Talk in the bath. Do you find the moment you take a bath, your daughter wants to join you? Often some of the best and most open conversations seem to take place in the tub. Kids can relax because they can see you are not going anywhere, and somehow the water and the lack of clothes just seem to invite more honest exchanges than you'd get at any other time.

Use the quiet time before bedtime. Another good time to talk is during the quiet time after lights out. In the same way as the water helps children relax, the darkness and lack of distractions also make them more open about their real concerns.

FOR OLDER GIRLS:
Be clear about how you feel. As your daughter gets older, some of the biggest misunderstandings will come not from how you treat her and feel about her, but from how she *thinks* you do. There may be a big gulf between the two. Leave her in no doubt about your feelings for her and how much you value her.

Keep hugging. After our children are too old to carry in our arms, somehow many of us fall out of the habit of having as much physical contact. But sometimes a bad mood, a strop, or a cry for attention can be cured with a hug. It can feel much more significant than words.

Keep talking. Even if you have said all the right things, your teenager may still appear to tune out much of what you have to say. But don't be discouraged. As JoAnn Deak, co-author of *Girls*

Will Be Girls: Raising Confident and Courageous Daughters, says: "Your Tween will believe you have no wisdom, but keep acting like you do. Your daughter will pretend she isn't listening to a word you are saying but keep talking because she is."[29]

Eat together. A fifth of Britons never eat together at the table. Instead, they eat in shifts and in front of the television. But as childcare educator Michael Grose points out: "That's a huge shame. It's no coincidence that those countries with a strong food culture also have strong families. When people eat together they talk. You can't help it when your behind is anchored to a chair."[30]

Check your body language. It's easy to assume that if we say the right words, our children will hear the right messages. But around 70 per cent of meaning is derived from non-verbal behaviour. Girls in particular pick up on every single cue we give them. They notice frowns and negative body language more than you think. So, instead of not looking up from your texts when she comes home from school, make sure your face really does light up. Use eye contact to show you are listening.

Check your tone. It's not just the words we speak that our children hear. It's also the tone in which we say them. One of the most corrosive is exasperation, which makes a child feel that not only is she a disappointment but that you have lost faith in her ability. Even if you are asking her to do something she should have done, or repeating yourself, speak in the same way you'd like to be spoken to.

Use humour. Some of the best parental communicators I know use laughter to defuse tension. Have family stories you retell. From a safe distance, find the funny side of things that have happened in the past.

How to answer tough questions children ask

If you want your daughter to be honest with you, you have to be honest with her. But what do you say when she asks questions which make you feel like a rabbit caught in the headlights, such as: "Why can't I say bad words if you can?" or "Did you ever take drugs?" There are plenty of questions that can leave us tongue-tied and fumbling for an answer. But remember that when kids ask you about your experiences with sex or drugs, they are not really asking about you, but themselves. Gauge what they know first, so you see how much they already understand – and what's age appropriate – before composing your answer.

What you can do:

Think carefully before you speak. Reflect the question back to your daughter and ask her what she means by it, to find out what's really on her mind.

Let her do most of the talking at first. Ask your daughter what she thinks the answer is. Find out how close her guess is to the truth, and just pause and listen. That way you will find out what question is really being asked.

Make difficult questions feel normal. Tell her that many kids her age have the same questions so that she does not feel alone with her worries.

PART 3

Growing up in the X-rated society

So far this book has set out to put both ourselves and our girls in the strongest position to fend off the damaging influences in today's society. Now here's what we're up against – and how to fight back.

Barely legal: what pornography does to children, and how to protect them

Because it's such a painful subject, parents prefer not to think about their children even seeing pornography. When I spoke to families, even those with much older teenage girls, most parents maintained their children were not "interested", hardly knew what pornography was, or would tell them if they saw anything disturbing.

It's a painful reality, but we live in a time when it's wildly optimistic to believe we can shield our girls completely, certainly by the time they are in secondary school. The hard truth is that it isn't a case of *if* your daughter will be exposed to pornography but *when*, according to the UK government's Sexualization of Children report.[31] In survey after survey, when questioned by adults who are not their parents, children admit to shocking levels of exposure. One in three has seen online pornography by the age of ten, according to a study by *Psychologies* magazine. Yet only half ever tell their parents.[32]

Parents are right, though, to guess that their girls don't go looking for pornographic material, or not at first. It comes and finds them. Indeed, among the younger girls I spoke to, many were aware there were "nasty pictures" out there and were anxious to avoid them. Pornography finds them via viral emails circulated by older children, pop-up ads, banners on websites, computer viruses, and phones. Others get a shock when they click on the wrong weblink, or misspell web addresses. According to the LSE study, nearly one in four have seen a pornographic pop-up advert while doing something else, almost as many have accidentally found themselves on a pornography site when looking for something else, and a quarter have been sent pornographic junk mail.[33]

But at the age of thirteen or fourteen, many girls' curiosity can become piqued. Older girls would only admit to seeing pornography at mates' houses, and said it was "funny" or "gross". But behind the dismissive attitude, they do seek it out to see what the fuss is all about, to find out what their friends are up to, to make sure they don't sound sexually naïve among their peer group – and even to get tips on what they think they should be doing.

Parents, however, remain remarkably innocent. Most I spoke to had no idea of the explicitness of the images easily accessible for free in seconds. Many believed that hard-core porn was still only to be found behind a safety curtain of pay walls – and that children needed credit card numbers to access it. But if the average young teenager, who has started to feel curious about what she hears, taps the word "sex" into Google, in less than a fifth of a second she will find herself looking into a kaleidoscope of thousands of video clips of the most extreme kind.

After all, pornography is a billion pound industry in Britain. According to the sociology professor Gail Dines, author of

Pornland, there are 420 million pornography pages, 4.2 million pornography websites, and 68 million internet searches for pornography every day. Around a third of all internet downloads are pornographic. "Sex" is the most searched word on the internet.[34] The market has become so competitive that pornographers now compete to provide more and more shocking images. What was once considered hard-core is now considered boring. You don't have to look very far to find women portrayed as if they enjoy being beaten, humiliated, and tied up, or even raped. But there are also images, immediately available, of women apparently in distress, forced to gag on penises, getting their faces covered with ejaculate, or being anally and vaginally penetrated by two or more men.

At first when children encounter pornography they don't realize they are watching fiction. There is so much of it – and it often claims to be real rather than staged – so they think it must be normal. Any curious young girl would quickly come to the conclusion that sex is a performance, not an act of emotional intimacy. Moreover many of the women in these images are identified as "barely legal" – in other words just sixteen – in order to get around child pornography laws. They are depicted as real teenage babysitters, cheerleaders, and schoolgirls. This tells children that they are already objects of lust, old enough to engage in any sexual activity going.

The problem is that it can take a lot to undo these damaging first impressions if children don't know any better. As Gail Dines says: "We know without a doubt that images you are exposed to impact the way you think about reality. It delivers a message in a crisp and succinct way – in your face, powerful and unambiguous: no morality, no empathy, no emotions outside anger."[35] The sex that our daughters hear so much about – and feel so much pressure to take part in – is shown as something brutal that men do to women. There is no kissing, no expressions of love or moments of tenderness. Women are casually referred to as cunts, sluts, and stupid bitches.

It's true that younger girls – under the age of about thirteen – will initially greet extreme images with repugnance. A survey by the Children's Digital Media Centre found that a quarter of young people who saw pornography initially felt "disgust, shock, or surprise". Other responses were anger, fear, and sadness. But gradually, it's clear that girls become desensitized and they start to view pornography as a particularly graphic kind of sex education.[36] At first, children may find these images upsetting, but go on to find them arousing, shameful, or both.[37] As they get older, more teenagers visit pornography sites. By the ages of fourteen to sixteen, four in every five children say they regularly access explicit photographs and footage on their home computers. Two-thirds view the same material on their mobile phones.

To date, there have been no long-term studies about how this exposure affects young minds. For obvious reasons, we can't expose children to explicit pornography and compare them with those who haven't viewed such images. However, there are snapshots of how pornography affects children's sexual behaviour. In 1994, 47 per cent of Grade 11 girls, aged around seventeen, in Canada said they'd had oral sex. With increasing internet use, the number had climbed to 52 per cent eight years later.[38] A 2008 University of Amsterdam study of nearly 2,400 Dutch teenagers found that more frequent exposure to explicit internet pornography was linked to their having a more open attitude to casual hook-ups and one-night stands, and a more "recreational" view of sex.[39] Among high school students in the US, 18 per cent of girls admitted actually doing some of the things sexually they had seen in pornography within a few days of viewing it, according to the Attorney General's Commission on Pornography. In the UK, too, 60 per cent of teenagers say pornography has affected their sex lives, according to a Channel 4 survey.[40]

At the moment, human sexual imprinting is not yet completely understood. But most psychologists agree that sexual fantasies and attachment to erotic objects are largely decided during certain periods in childhood development. How much pornography affects each person will depend on what developmental stage they are at, and their underlying temperament and life experiences. But given the hundreds of studies linking TV violence to real life violence over the last thirty years, it would be naïve to believe that pornography has no effect. Just as internet sex is changing the way adults behave in the bedroom, it will change how children eventually behave too. Once anal sex was a minority activity for heterosexuals. But the internet has made it normal – and among young women most of all. The latest survey shows that 20 per cent of US eighteen- to nineteen-year-old girls have had anal sex, double the number for women twenty years ago.[41]

While most of my generation learned what they enjoyed in bed through trial and error, girls are having their sexual identities foisted on them before they've had a boyfriend, or know what's appropriate in a healthy sexual relationship. Fetishes, developed over time by adults and often far removed from loving relationships, have become seen as the norm by our children, who don't know any better. But although we may not yet know the full outcome of porn on girls' deepest sexual identity, the plethora and heartlessness of porn is certainly affecting what they think is expected of them – and how far they think they should go.

Several of the young girls I speak to admit they are already taking part in more casual relationships. They are more likely to see sex as a meaningless pastime done in the moment, not as part of ongoing relationships with "someone special". The longer they view pornography, the more they also start to view it as an animated sex education course. In short, it becomes their template for how they think they are supposed to behave. According to a study of teens in California, half of girls who have seen porn say they have learned "a lot."

This is compounded by the fact that girls have come to confuse female empowerment with sexual aggressiveness. They think behaving like a porn star makes them look sexy, confident, and sophisticated in the same way as a pop star only wearing a bra is seen as confident and in control. As a result, the word "slut" has become a form of praise. A search for user names using the word "slut" on Bebo returned more than 30,000 results.

The first generation of young women to be exposed to pornography at its current level of pervasiveness are now coming to recognize how bad this early exposure was for them. In a poll for the book *Pornified*, it's the eighteen- to twenty-four-year-olds who are most in favour of measures to regulate pornography. Four out of ten in this age group believe pornography damages relationships, compared to three out of ten twenty-five- to forty-year-olds, who haven't seen as much of it. As the author Pamela Paul says: "The internet generation is also more likely to believe that pornography changes men's expectations of women's looks and behaviour."[42]

Furthermore, we need to ask how pornography is affecting the generation of boys our daughters will one day meet. The psychologist Gary Brooks, author of *The Centrefold Syndrome*, believes that pornographic images make men think they need to have a variety of sexual partners and they stop them from finding true intimacy with one woman. He says: "Boys learn that they become men by desiring strangers, women they don't even know. They don't learn to feel comfortable in relationships with real girls."[43] Who can say how much heartache and how many broken relationships these attitudes may lead to for our daughters in years to come?

And what of the present, and how it affects the attitude of adults to children? In one video on pornhub.com, one of the most popular pornography websites, a man is seen having sex with a flat-chested young woman with be-ribboned bunches who is identified as "the slut from *The Brady Bunch*". In the 1970s sit-com, Cindy Brady was seven years old.

What you can do:

FOR YOUNGER GIRLS:

Set up filters. Although the British government has asked internet service providers to look at ways to limit the free availability of pornography, legislation is still a long way off. In any case, parents have to face up to the fact that they are the first line of defence, and that however uninterested they think their child is, it's better to be safe. The good news is that most of the time content filters are already built into phones, computers, and search engines, so it's often much easier than parents think to switch them on. The safeguards won't work indefinitely, especially if your daughter becomes intent on bypassing them. But they can save a younger girl getting a nasty shock she is not ready for.

Tell them what to do if they see something that scares them. If your daughter sees something nasty or disturbing, tell her she won't get into trouble. Show her how to close the web-browser or simply turn off the screen and make sure she tells a grown-up. Another option is to download Hector's World Safety Button (from http://www.thinkuknow.co.uk), which then sits in the top right-hand corner of the screen. It will cover an offending image or message until you come and remove it.

FOR OLDER GIRLS:

Explain that pornography is not "real" sex. Take the initiative and tell your daughter that pornography is out there, before she comes across it for herself. Tell her pornography is not sex, in the way that a thriller or action movie is not what happens in real life. It's grown-ups play-acting for the camera and it ignores the real purpose of sex, which is to feel closer to someone we love. Real sex is about intimacy and the pleasure of the two people doing it and it requires emotion and affection. Pornography is for the entertainment of the person watching.

Don't believe your child won't eventually be exposed to it.
Just because you're vigilant doesn't mean other parents will be.
Even if your child does not see porn in your home, there's a good
chance she will be introduced to it by her peers or older siblings.
That's why it's so important to keep talking. Cover all the bases,
too. On average children have at least three different methods of
access to the internet, so setting up internet filters on your main
family computer still won't be enough.

Don't over-react. If you discover that your daughter has been
watching pornography, don't tell her off, or she'll never discuss
it with you again. Talk to her: many teenagers don't tell their
parents about what they've seen because they're "worried about
the reaction".[44]

Support regulation. Back British government moves towards
blocking pornography websites, unless adults "opt in" to view
them. After all, internet service providers have been able to
control child pornography after pressure from government,
and gambling websites are also all age-restricted. So, however
technically difficult it may be, support moves to ask ISPs to go
a step further so pornography is not freely available for children
to stumble across. The idea is backed by a growing number of
psychologists and doctors. Write to your MP and support the
safer media campaign at www.mediamarch.org.uk.

Sex education

"Even though my daughters are seventeen and thirteen, I have never had the big conversation with them. If I did, they'd just raise their eyes to heaven, and say they know it all anyway. I suppose I've never really stopped to think about where from, although they have had some talks and films from school. I suppose I am being a bit naïve. I just don't want to discuss that sort of thing with them."
Celia, 40

Telling children about sex is often a conversation parents prefer to put off until the very last moment. Many parents don't bother because as soon as they bring it up, their daughters tell them they know it all anyway. As one mother told me: "If I try to discuss it, my fourteen-year-old daughter just rolls her eyes and says: 'Why are you telling me now? It's a bit late!'" In fact, 40 per cent of teenagers have intercourse before they've even discussed safe sex with their parents.[45] A recent Unicef survey of twenty-one countries also found that British children were the most likely to have had sex before the age of fifteen. Sexually transmitted infections in Britain have risen by 63 per cent in a decade, with HIV and gonorrhoea close to record levels.[46]

What you can do:

Focus on the emotional side. Don't just issue dire warnings about sex, as this will only make it sound more exciting and forbidden. Put the emphasis on patience, trust, affection, and pleasure.

Ask her if he's really the one who deserves her. If you feel your child is about to lose her virginity, it's pointless trying to forbid her. If she's not yet in a long-term or meaningful relationship, ask her if she really wants to open up her body to someone who hasn't proved his loyalty or love for her.

Ask her to take her time. Tell her it's fine to keep talking about sex with her friends, and finding out more, but she can't take back losing her virginity – and you don't want it to be a disappointment for her. Tell her sex is meant to be fun and intimate, not embarrassing and painful. Question if she wouldn't prefer to reach a stage with a lover where she can be open enough to say what she enjoys.

Suggest she makes sure she is doing it for the right reasons. Does she really want to have sex – or does she just want to be able to tell her mates? Explain that hormones, peer pressure, and alcohol may all lead her to choose the wrong moment. If she really has found a boy she wants to sleep with, tell her to wait a few weeks or months to make sure none of these factors are influencing her decision. If he's the right one, he'll wait.

Bring back love. As one teacher told me: "Sex isn't a big deal any more in the same way it was in our day. They don't even think they have to be in a relationship." It's very sad that young girls are separating love and sex so early on, so make sure you stress the link. Whatever they may say, the idea of waiting for someone you love still appeals to teenage girls. It sounds obvious, but remind her she is much more than a female body to have sex with.

Best friends and worst enemies: helping your daughter cope with peer pressure

"I have just started secondary school and I am not sure what popular means any more. I used to think it meant you are a person that lots of people like because you are nice. But at my new school it seems to mean that your parents are rich, and that you are pretty and thin."
Vanessa, 11

"If I went up to the popular group at school, they'd giggle and walk off. It's because I've got spots. It's really brutal."
Anya, 12

"They all have labels for themselves according to what they look like – there's the spotty ones, the geeky ones, the fat ones, the pretty ones. It's much more defined than it was in my day."
Joanna, mother, 39

"In my child's group at school, there's something called the Ace Gang. They are the clique of the richest, prettiest girls in the class. In other words the self-styled 'beautiful people'. They are all on the skinny side with straight hair and the most stylish clothes – and they nearly all date older boys at the nearby boys' school. I was absolutely horrified when I found out this clique actually had a name, which seemed to imply everyone else was inferior. I was even more shocked when I spoke to a mum at another school in the area, who said there was an Ace Gang in her child's class, too. It's like these girls are trying to create a new class of super-perfect beings."
Rosalind, mother, 44

The role of friendship

When the Children's Society asked children what made their childhood happy, friendship was the thing they mentioned most often.[47] For a girl, having friends with whom she can be herself is probably the most important factor in making her feel good about herself, and in making her want to go to school. Having a circle of playmates helps a child see that she is likeable to the outside world. It builds her self-esteem because she knows friendship is a choice. Further into the future, the relationship lessons she learns in her tween years also help her choose healthy adult relationships.

From the other side of the school gates, it often feels as though we have to leave our children to it. Yet, even from the outside, we can still help children to identify healthy friendships that are supportive and helpful and which prepare them for the future.

Good friends and bad friends

Natalie Collins of Faith and Freedom, who leads seminars to teach young children aged seven and up about healthy relationships, poses the following questions to help them learn who's a good friend and who's not.

A BAD FRIEND IS SOMEONE WHO:
- doesn't want me to play with other friends;
- tells me that what I like is stupid;
- laughs at me;
- makes me feel sad;
- pushes me to do things I don't want to;
- thinks they are better than me;
- hurts me;
- says they will do something unkind to me if I do not do what they want;
- tells people my secrets;
- tells me my friends don't like me.

A GOOD FRIEND IS SOMEONE WHO:
- plays with all my friends;
- tells me I am good at doing stuff;
- doesn't mind if I don't want to do stuff;
- I have lots of fun with;
- I don't have to play with all the time;
- Doesn't insist I have to like all the same things they do;
- Doesn't require me to do anything to stay being their friend.

What you can do:

FOR YOUNGER GIRLS:

Organize play-dates. There are some mothers who don't make this a priority, often because a child is their second or third, or because they don't have the time or the inclination. Yet the more your daughter is able to role-play and pretend, the more she will be able to decode the emotions of others and "read" them. You will also be able to develop friendships with other mothers whose values about child-rearing chime with yours.

Don't be a helicopter parent. In the early days, play-dates are the cement that builds friendships. But don't hover over your child and her playmates. Give them space to feel comfortable with each other. A study by the psychologist John Gottman found that creative, imaginative play is central to friendship, but it quickly stops once parents burst the play bubble.[51]

Try to see life from your daughter's point of view. Remember how important your friendships were at school. Do you recall how it felt when one of your friends inexplicably stopped talking to you? Or the mortification when you had no one to play with at break? Remember that her friendships will feel like life or death to her. Of course, as an adult you can see the wider picture, and you know that you survived. But at the moment your daughter is very much stuck in the microcosm of school, which can be a claustrophobic place. Take all her concerns seriously.

Tell her not to take differences of opinion personally. Your child can come home in tears simply because another girl said she didn't like her favourite pop star. These sorts of remarks are attempts by other girls to work out who's allowed in their group and who isn't, which is why differences of opinion get taken so seriously. Even so, you will be encouraging your daughter to be an individual if you tell her that everyone is entitled to her own views.

Check her TV viewing. The effects of exclusion-based TV programmes are trickling down to younger children all the time. Children also grow up on a diet of humour from programmes that are often too old for them and often consist of one insult after another. Keep programmes age appropriate.

Tell her never to expect to have just one perfect best friend. Explain that no one person can meet all her needs and that she should build a circle of friends, each with something different to offer.

Explain that friendship problems are inevitable. Don't pretend that everything will be rosy in the playground. Explain, before they happen, that bust-ups are an inevitable part of life, and friendships don't always last forever. Talk about fallings out you've had with your friends, what caused them, and how they turned out.

Don't wait until it's too late. If you wait until your child is already excluded or bullied after a playground row, it's too late. She's already too upset to listen to your advice to stand up for herself. Instead of allowing her to cast herself as the victim, teach her how to be assertive without being aggressive. Get her to role-play dealing with difficult playground scenarios, such as a friend who won't let her play with another friend. It may not come naturally to her, but at least you are giving her the tools to handle these situations positively.

Teach her that everyone has feelings. If you build empathy in your child she is less likely to bully. Tell your children to be friendly and polite to peers, whether they are friends or not.

Teach her that questions can be the best defence. Teach your child to have the confidence to question why another girl is saying hurtful things. Tell her simply to ask: "Why are you saying that?"

or "What's your point?" Many girls will back off when asked to account for their remarks.

Get older kids to help. One of the most under-used resources we have is the help of older siblings, cousins, or friends who have recently navigated the stormy water of peer-group relationships and can act as mentors. Just talking to them helps younger children realize they're not alone.

Look at your own behaviour. As one teacher told me: "Nasty mums often have the nastiest children." Ask yourself if you are bitching and gossiping at the school gate. If your child hears you judging and undermining others she will quickly learn to do the same, even if you think it's going over her head. Think twice, too, about reading gossip magazines, and turn off bitchy TV programmes.

Explain that nastiness will ultimately make your daughter feel bad about herself. Studies have found that people who bitch and gossip suffer lower self-esteem afterwards, while those who are kind and generous to others feel better about their whole selves. Remind her that unkind remarks say more about the person making them than they do about the victim.

Tell her that bullying is more than just hitting. Explain that ignoring people, leaving them out, pulling faces, and using a sarcastic tone of voice are also bullying. It doesn't matter how "annoying" she judges another child to be, it's never justified.

Don't enable cliques. In primary schools, where mothers often try to help forge their children's friendships, sometimes class cliques get actively encouraged. Mums can tend to organize play-dates with other children based on whether the other child comes from a family they approve of. By all means gravitate towards parents with similar values, but also check that you are not trying to engineer your child's friendships based on what size house or make of car the other child's family has. Encourage your daughter to mix with a good range of boys and girls her own age.

FOR OLDER GIRLS:
Talk to your daughter about the power of the clique. Explain that people often seek out cliques because they feel insecure or crave the protection of the group. Talk to her about your experiences at school and how you fitted in, and stress that her individuality is always more important. Tell her how being in a clique can limit her and cut her off from other people who could be good friends.

Don't encourage "queen bee" behaviour. Mothers who were – or are – used to being the centre of attention themselves secretly may quite like seeing their girls being in the most exclusive cliques. If you are that mother, break the cycle, because your daughter's individuality is worth more than that.

Talk about gossip. Discuss with your child how easy it is to be carried away by the intrigue and drama of a new nugget of information. Ask them if they think it's really all right to pass on gossip about someone else, how they would feel if the gossip was about them, and what they are really gaining from it.

Tell her that putting herself down won't make her more popular. Some girls think that by putting themselves down they will seem less threatening and more likeable to their peers. Explain that at best it will make people feel sorry for her. At worst, they will dismiss or take advantage of her. It certainly won't win her more friends, because people like people who like themselves.

Give her outlets outside school. Social circles inside schools can be fraught with power politics, so give her an outlet outside school so her classroom friendships are not the be-all and end-all. This means that if she has a social hiccup at school, she still has the security of knowing there are people out there who know and like her.

Ask what your school is doing. Many schools seem to accept cliques as an inevitable part of life. But cliques can poison the atmosphere and divide year groups into winners and losers. Ask what your school is doing to develop kids' healthy friendships. Do teachers seem aware of developing situations? Do they have a circle time or a discussion forum so that girls realize they are not alone with their friendship worries? Some schools also give children mentors from older classes and organize "mix it up days" when pupils spend lunch sitting next to someone they don't know.

Explain that friendship is a matter of taste and timing. Just because your daughter perceives she does not have as many friends as others doesn't make her an unlikeable person. Friendship is also a question of meeting the right people at the right time, and just because she's not "popular" now doesn't mean she won't have lots of good friends in the future.

Take back the word "popularity". Explain that true popularity is having friends who like her for who she is, and liking herself. Explain the difference between good popularity, which is based on the individual, and bad popularity, which is based on fashion, looks, and status. Don't let her think that because she is not in the popular group, she is not a valuable person.

Don't use the silent treatment. Children who use the silent treatment, threaten not to be friends, and give others the cold shoulder most likely picked up the behaviour from their parents, according to a study by Brigham Young University. Researchers have found that parents who attempt to control their children by manipulating the child–parent bond have kids who treat their friends the same way. Be a role model even in the most subtle ways you treat others.[52]

Arm her with coping strategies. Your daughter may find it hard to get out of situations she's not happy with while still looking "cool" in front of the clique. She may not want to take drugs or alcohol, but may find herself swept up in the moment and not know how to get out of the situation. Teach her some ways of escaping while still saving face, such as shifting the responsibility for the decision to you, or using humour or diversion. If she's willing, help her practise with role-play.

Ask her to listen to her values. Ask your daughter to recognize when something she is asked to do by her friends conflicts with what she feels is right. Tell her never to respond to a "dare" – which is inevitably someone else trying to persuade her to do something dangerous they would get into trouble for. Explain that being a true friend is about wanting the best for a friend, not the worst.

Teach her to practise saying no to peers. If she's older, tell her that always saying yes doesn't make people like her more or make her a better friend. Explain that not wanting to be different or cause a fuss might lead her to do things she isn't comfortable with. Tell her she will get more respect from peers if she trusts her own judgment.

Bullying

No matter how many anti-bullying policies are in place in schools, there will be times when your daughter will face cruelty from other girls – or indeed may inflict it. Very few girls are lucky enough to escape completely. Nasty remarks which were once made in the heat of the moment and then forgotten about are now set in stone on Facebook or in text messages, where they can fester, drag in others, and sometimes turn into full-scale classroom feuds. Girls' developing judgment can also falter because they can say something while remaining hidden behind the safety of a computer screen. Messages can get misinterpreted and rumours spread. Exclusion from parties and sleepovers becomes all too obvious when pictures of the event get posted on the internet. As one parent told me: "They just don't think what they are doing."

Feuds can sometimes go on for weeks without parents having an inkling. Too often girls say nothing because they are terrified by the prospect of your wading in and humiliating them. Your daughter may also panic because she's the one who has to face the other girls day in, day out, not you. Her ideal solution is for the problem magically to disappear.

In this fraught and combustible environment, it's imperative that parents warn girls long before a quarrel happens. Don't leave it until she is in tears because her friend has called her a "fat slag". By then she will be too hurt and distraught to listen to you. Even before you need to, tell her that cruelty and meanness are often due to insensitivity, insecurity, lapses of judgment, and aspects of human behaviour that are hard to control. She isn't necessarily to blame.

What you can do:

Don't assume your daughter's an angel. Almost all the mothers I spoke to whose girls were involved in cyber-scraps said it was never, ever their daughters' fault. But, of course, they would think that because they've only heard their child's side of the story – the one designed to portray her in the best light. Often it's hard to get to the bottom of who said what to whom.

Ask your daughter to record what's been said. If your daughter is seriously under attack from a cyber-bully, it will help her feel more empowered to print off or write down the times and dates of the comments. It will also make her think twice about sending messages back that will inflame the situation. If needs be, this will help her school to intervene.

Help her stand up for herself. If your daughter makes it clear she's not going to be pushed around, the bullies will quickly move on to easier targets. They might even become amicable – long-term feuds benefit no one. Work out a script that helps your daughter confront the other girl, and look for a way to smooth over what's happened.

The power of the clique

Up until the age of around eight, friendships are relatively uncomplicated. Girls often play in fluid and loosely formed groups of five or six, with perhaps a best friend within the group. Then, around Year Four, girls tend to start to want to pick and choose, and more clearly defined friendship groups start to form. The first lines may start to be drawn when a girl no longer wants to invite her whole class to her birthday parties and starts to select preferred friends for sleepovers. But of course our best friends can also be our worst enemies.

Inevitably, your younger daughter will come home distraught that a friend refused to sit together at lunch, didn't let her have the role she wanted in a game, or even said her name in the wrong tone of voice. As she grows older, much of this interaction becomes so subtle as to be imperceptible to the adult eye. But fears that others are whispering about her, or sighing, tutting, or raising their eyes around her, can bring a girl's world crashing down. This is a normal part of growing up, but that doesn't make it easier for you – or her – to deal with. So start preparing her early.

As your child grows, the walls of friendship groups get higher, like fortresses designed to protect them during the insecure years of puberty and to exclude everyone else. By the time your daughter is about twelve, if not earlier, friends will be the main influence on how she talks, what she likes, how she dresses, and her ideas about how she fits in. And though we all had friendship groups when we were growing up, the lines now seem to have become much more rigid in today's schools.

More than ever, British schools are more like their US counterparts, with clearly defined "popular cliques" at the top of the pile. While boys will form themselves into friendship groups according to sports, musical taste, or hobbies, girls tend to define themselves by a mixture of wealth, looks, likes, fashion, beauty, and precociousness. The need to be popular and to be viewed as the "in crowd" has become so imperative that the dominant popular groups now give themselves names – such as Ace Gang – to confirm their social dominance.

If unchecked, the exclusion and the bullying that some cliques foster can infect the whole class, making the outsiders feel like losers. Yet even within the security of the clique, there is insecurity. As Rosalind Wiseman points out in *Queen Bees and Wannabes*, the trading of secrets, jealousy, and competition mean that every girl feels she has to watch her back. Power plays within the group are likely to be such that she has to fight to stay a member by wearing the right clothes and saying the right things.[48] It doesn't help that among girls who have been exposed to "reality TV" there is a tendency for bitchy, excluding, and judgmental behaviour to flare up even sooner. On such programmes adults are in ongoing competition with their peers to be the winners of a popularity contest, and are regularly seen judging others, back-stabbing, scheming, and plotting. It's not surprising that friendship is seen by young minds as a disposable commodity, used as a means to an end.

Peer pressure is likely to be a key factor in how soon your daughter decides to have sex and whether she drinks or takes drugs. The risk is that if she gets too deeply immersed in a clique a girl may lose her individuality and take decisions to impress them rather than be true to herself. The frustration for parents is that girls will always listen to their best friends, no matter how damaging their influence. As Rosalind Wiseman points out: "No matter what they do to her, she still feels her friends know her best and want what is best for her."[49]

But even if your daughter seems no longer to care about what you have to say, state your case anyway if you think she's making a bad decision. She won't want to admit it, but what you think is still important to her. Even if she always defends her friends, there will have been moments when they put her in an uncomfortable position and encouraged her to act against her values. So deep down she will know perfectly well what you are talking about. Your message still has the chance of getting through, even if it's met by eye-rolling or denial.

In the best case scenario, you will have helped your daughter's self-esteem grow so strong already that she will have enough emotional intelligence to know her own mind. She will avoid exclusive cliques altogether and choose her friends on the basis of who they are, not on their image. In a typical group of school children, 35 per cent belong to a "popular group", 45 per cent are in the average group – not popular but with a handful of close friends – and 10 per cent have few or no friends, according to studies by social scientists.[50] The safest place for your daughter is charting the middle way.

Abusive relationships

The targeting of young girls by gangs of youths for sex is the latest effect of early sexualization to hit the headlines. Girls desperate to appear older than they are prove easy prey for groups of young men. Openly available pornography depicting "barely legal" teenagers, with braces on their teeth and pigtails, encourages them to see young girls as sexually available. And the huge number of videos on the net showing gang sex send out still more unhealthy messages that group intercourse with girls is a legitimate hobby for young men.

All this is horrifying for parents who, thanks to girls' excellent secret-keeping skills, often have no idea of what their daughters might be caught up in. The easiest targets for abuse will always be girls with low self-esteem, looking for someone to flatter and "protect" them, who find out too late what this actually entails. But whether or not your daughter falls into this category – and even if she is never threatened with violence or rape – you will still be providing her with a lifetime of insight if you show her how to tell the difference between a healthy and an unhealthy relationship. Don't leave it too late. Girls are getting into sexual relationships sooner than ever. And controlling behaviour by young men can begin at any age, so start having the conversation as soon as you notice she's taking an interest in the opposite sex that might lead to a relationship. Even relatively young teenage boys, egged on by brutal pornography, can try to assume dominant positions.

Just as you can teach her the difference between a good friend and a bad friend in the playground, discuss the difference between a good and a bad "romantic" relationship. She may never come across anyone manipulative or abusive, but she should be warned. Above all, emphasize that you are her safety net, and whatever she has got involved in, or however embarrassing the outcome, she should never feel too ashamed or frightened to come to you.

Former probation officer Pat Craven tours the country talking to young girls in schools. In her work, she points out the warning signs that will enable girls to spot "dominators" – not just in gangs but in everyday relationships. This is not just about extreme cases in which a girl gets raped or abused. If a boyfriend makes her feel uneasy, makes her keep secrets, or sulks to get his own way, then tell your daughter she should walk away rather than be dragged in deeper.

It is also fundamental that parents don't feed their girls myths that can be turned against them, says Pat. If girls feel that they are little princesses, whose place it is to be protected and showered with material things, it is easy for them to start being controlled and made to feel they "owe" something. Pat says: "Young girls are falling into a pattern of abuse because they are still getting the message that it's a woman's place to be dominated by a man. For example, don't let them think it's romantic for their boyfriend to be texting them forty times a day."

As girls get older and start to learn more about adult relationships, they also need to be adult enough to decide for themselves. Pat says: "Print out the list of differences between 'Mr Wrong' and 'Mr Right', stick it on the fridge for them to read, and ask them to work it out. But if we don't tell girls the warning signs, we could be letting them sleepwalk into bad relationships – with a lifetime of consequences."[53]

Wired children:
from sexting to Facebook

"Young girls are having such a nightmare about their appearance – and feel so bad about themselves that when some random bloke posts a Facebook comment saying: 'You're gorgeous', or 'You're hot', you feel flattered. When you're growing up and not sure how you look, it's what you want to hear. Common sense easily goes out of the window."
Issy, veteran Facebook user, 23

"My daughter had a really nasty falling out on Facebook with a girl she had been best friends with since she was six. The reason was really trivial and it would have blown over if it hadn't then been exaggerated out of all proportion when it was played out for everyone to see on Facebook. All the other girls in the class started getting involved. It turned into a show of bravado too as the girls started calling each other 'bitch' and 'slut' for everyone to see. She never told me while it was happening, although I did notice that my daughter was withdrawn and preoccupied. It was only when I asked why I hadn't seen the other girl around that she admitted what was going on – and even then I only got the full story from another mum in the class."
Judith, mother, 35

On a bed emblazoned with Hello Kitties, thirteen-year-old Natasha jokily poses for her best friend's mobile phone camera. With one knee on the bed and the other off, she raises her bottom in the air and looks round at the lens with a pout, accentuated by the red feather boa around her neck. Natasha likes what she sees. You can't see her spots and her face looks thinner when she twists around. So she posts it as her profile picture on Facebook, where a dozen of her 400-odd friends rush to post comments such as "Oooh, nice one!" and "Sexeeeee!"

A click away, her twelve-year-old friend Beth is also getting the idea, and has just posed for her new profile picture. Last week the photo she felt best summed her up was a shot of her riding a pony at a recent horse trial, and before that one with her friends in a huddle on a school geography field trip. This week, the image she wants to present is one she took of herself in the mirror with her hips angled to show off the snug fit of her Daisy Duke shorts, matched with a tankini and a cowboy hat.

Even as adults, we project our ideal image of ourselves on Facebook – the side we most want people to see. It's a statement of what we think is important about us. You only have to comb through the sites of a few of today's young girls, many of whom look like soft porn stars in training, to see how many of them want to be thought of as sexy. They soon find out that the sexier they are on Facebook, and the more they share about themselves, the more comments and friends they attract.

Of course, growing girls have always posed for pictures like these. What woman hasn't got a faintly embarrassing picture of herself getting ready for the school disco and pouting as she tried to find what being "sexy" looks like? The problem is that our children's embarrassing moments are now posted forever in cyberspace for hundreds of people to see. For our daughters, these pictures are their signature. But they can also end up creating cyber-sex versions of themselves that they then feel pressure to live up to in real life.

The truth is that girls strike these poses for each other as much as for boys. All often goes well at first. But if a girl is seen as too sexy or too hot by her peers, eventually the snaps attract negative comments which can cause her teetering self-image to fall off a cliff. But unfortunately it's not just her peers who will be looking. Girls can be very susceptible to flattery, even from people they don't really know. When all you want to know is whether you're pretty, when someone comes on and tells you that you're gorgeous, it's hard not to listen. Facebook gives growing girls the fantasy that they are in control of their image, and how it is used, when they are not.

According to the Child Exploitation and Online Protection Centre (CEOP), the sexier girls look in their pictures the more likely they are to be targeted by adult predators. The latest figures show that in 2010 the organization received 6,291 reports, a rise of 880 on the previous year.[54] More than 400 of these were about men asking girls to live up to their image by performing sex acts. Another 1,500 were reports of perpetrators storing or spreading the images. At the thin end of the wedge, in 513 cases girls ended up meeting people they had contacted online, and being abused.

Rolling through these Facebook pictures, what is so poignant is how soon girls start to reminisce about their lost childhood. Between the seductive images are pictures of primary school line-ups and nursery school birthday parties. It's as if the pressure for sexualization is already making thirteen- and fourteen-year-olds nostalgic for a simpler life.

But as they play and interact in person less and less in the real world, Facebook is far from being an ideal alternative, especially considering that recent surveys have found that teens are spending between an hour and a half and two hours each day on social network sites. Yet parents have told me that, along with mobile phones, Facebook is the most difficult thing to say no to. Many gave in because of constant nagging, or from the fear that their children would lose out socially. Most only monitored their Facebook use for the first few months, and were mainly worried about predators, but ran out of time and stopped checking their daughters' accounts when they felt reassured this wasn't happening. Few even bothered to monitor Bebo or Twitter because they didn't consider them risks.

Parents often mutter about respecting their child's privacy. But by its very nature, Facebook is not a private place – it's a public space shared by millions of people, so the dangers are magnified. It would be as wrong to let your daughter wander through it on her own and without guidance, as it would be to let her drive on a motorway without having taken a driving test.

By all means use a light touch, keep a low profile and back off as much as possible until she's been on it a few years and has proved she knows how to handle herself. But the problems associated with Facebook tend to crop up so quickly and are so devastating, you need to be there to help her handle them.

What you can do:

Join Facebook yourself. The only way really to understand how Facebook and other social networking sites work is to join. You don't have to participate, but you need to be present. Certainly at the start, tell your daughter that one of the conditions of signing up is that she makes you a friend. If she wants to block you, ask why. If it's because she is embarrassed by you being there, offer to go on under a different name. Be open about your involvement from the start. It's essential she maintains her trust in you.

Keep a boundary around Facebook. Teenagers can get so addicted to Facebook that they'd rather post messages all day than actually go out there and meet and talk to people. Of course your child needs to be in touch with her friends, but be ready to point out if her Facebook use is distorting or distracting from real face-to-face relationships.

Explain what a real friend is. Tell your daughter that having friends on Facebook is not the same as having real friends. Tell her only to add people as friends if she really knows them, and not to accept anyone just because they know people in common.

Set Facebook security settings on high. Ask her to make sure she is only Facebook friends with people whose lives she wants to share – and who she wants to share hers. Suggest she opens up her page to close family and friends only.

Fight your corner on Facebook. Many parents argue that they should back off and leave Facebook to their children because reading their pages is like reading their diaries. But the stakes are much higher because lapses in judgment can quickly escalate into real-world problems such as bullying and inappropriate behaviour. A remark in a diary is private and easily forgotten. An ill-judged post or picture on Facebook goes much further, is seen by hundreds, and can be difficult to remove.

Warn your daughter that she will get left out. Probably the most hurtful effect of Facebook is when girls see pictures of parties they were not invited to. It leaves them feeling excluded, unpopular, yet unable to say anything. Prepare her that this is likely to happen, that not everyone gets invited to everything. Ask her to be thoughtful when posting her own photos.

Discourage honesty boxes. There are Facebook applications, amazingly, which invite anonymous comments. Girls hold out for praise from secret admirers, but are too often devastated when they get something nasty and hurtful and have no idea who it's from.

Warn her about cyber-bullying before it happens. Don't wait. Warn your daughter that, unfortunately, it's quite likely someone will post something unpleasant or untrue, even though it's not a reflection on her. Tell her how pervasive the problem is, and, at the same time, make it clear you expect her never to add to the problem by posting something cruel or insulting herself.

Give her a mental checklist. Remind her that what she means to say may be read differently by other people. If for one moment she hears a voice in her head saying: "Is this a good idea?" tell her this is a good clue that it's probably not.

Tell them who's watching. Remind your girls that the internet is a public forum and the material they post can be seen by other parents, teachers, or future employers. Once they've been posted, pictures and comments can go anywhere – and never be taken back.

Drawing up an internet safety promise

Before your daughter has become so deeply immersed that these promises are redundant, sit down together and work out a set of boundaries that she agrees will keep her safe. She may not stick to every rule, but at least you've set her off thinking about the issues.

- If I see anything online that upsets me, I'll tell my parents.
- If I'm not sure a website is OK, I will ask first.
- I won't give any personal information, such as my real name, address, age, phone number, school, passwords, or what I look like, to anyone online.
- I won't send pictures without permission.
- I will get my parents' approval before filling in forms for competitions, surveys, or services.
- I won't write or forward threatening, unkind emails, instant messages, or postings on websites or blogs – even anonymously.
- I won't answer emails or instant messages from someone I do not know.
- I won't arrange to meet anyone in person or phone anyone that I meet online without my parents' permission. I know that people may not be who they say they are online.
- I won't install software without my parents' knowledge. File sharing programs such as Kazaa, Limewire, or BearShare are not allowed.
- I will stick to these rules whether I am at home, at a friend's house, or on my phone. If I break them, I know I may lose the right to use technology.

Getting technical

While we are reluctant to see our children step beyond the garden gate on their own, in cyberspace we grant them their independence early. According to the Home Office sexualization report, 99 per cent of eight- to seventeen-year-olds have access to the internet; and 60 per cent of twelve- to fifteen-year-olds say that they mostly use it on their own. Almost half say that their parents set no rules for internet use.[55]

Filters are certainly under-used. But even if we switch them all on, older kids who want to bypass them usually can. It can become a game of subterfuge we can't win. More than six out of ten say they know how to hide what they do online from their parents. Nearly a third of teenagers clear the browser history when they log off, and one in six has created private email addresses or social networking profiles.[56] As one mother told me: "My daughter just laughs at me because she knows so much more than me." As long ago as 2005, 32 per cent of children considered themselves advanced internet users, compared with 16 per cent of grown-ups. So if we leave our daughter to navigate the internet on her own, we open the door to a virtual world where we can't accompany her. Once she passes through, we can't check the TV listings to see what she will be watching. She can travel into whatever realms she likes. The internet becomes her own lawless private world where adults have no place.

So we have to keep the conversation going, and stay present in our children's lives. We shouldn't abandon them to technology because it keeps them quiet and makes life easier for us. If we do allow them total freedom, there's no way of telling how far they will go.

What you can do:

FOR YOUNGER GIRLS:

Surf with them. Younger kids are likely to be pleased and excited to have you surfing along with them to start with. Help them find a selection of sites they like, and file them in their favourites list. Ask them to log on to those favourites when you're not with them. Most girls under the age of ten are happy to stick with what they already know.

Place limits early. If you give children unlimited access to the internet and computers from the start, they regard it as a right, not a privilege, that should be available to them around the clock – and that's very hard to claw back. From early on, limit use to half an hour using a timer so you don't face endless negotiations for extensions. Set a designated time every day, but make it only after homework, music practice, or chores are done.

Tell them never to give out information. Tell girls never to give out any information at all about themselves without your permission. Good sites or people who know them don't need to ask how old they are, where they live, or what they look like.

Give them safe search engines. Google and Yahoo are amazing resources, but the access they give to children is just too huge. Give them a list of kids' search engines such as Kidsclick (kidsclick.org), Looksmart kids (search.netnanny.com), and Ask Jeeves for Kids (www.ajkids.com). They are fun, written in simple language, and, best of all, no pornographic or sexual content will come up, even if they were to ask for it.

Be with them when they use YouTube. YouTube is a great educational resource, but the recommended videos that appear on the right-hand side of the screen can quickly branch off into unpleasant territory. For example, the funny animal videos that tween girls love can quickly divert into subject areas that are more disturbing. Switch on the safety mode in the lower left-hand corner of the screen. It takes just minutes.

Don't let your child have a computer in her room. Always insist that the computer she is using is in a public place in the home, where it can be seen and shared by the whole family. This is not fail safe, but there's less chance your child will be tempted to browse for something unsuitable if you might wander past at any moment. Agree that if you see her clicking away from something when you come close then you have the right to see what it is.

Use your computer's inbuilt security settings. This is probably much, much easier than you imagined. Many security settings are already available on your computer and just need to be enabled. They won't give protection forever, but will certainly help save children from stumbling on something they are not ready for.

Teach scepticism. Children are naïve. They start off taking everything they read on the internet at face value. But then this is hardly surprising when so many schools recommend using internet research for homework. Teach your daughter that information on the web is not always reliable. Help her ask questions. Ask her to work out who created a site and what it's for. For example, does it have a logo or does it say what the sources of the information are? Can she tell if it's based on opinion or fact?

Explain that not all sites are the same. While they are still young, most girls don't want to come across scary or explicit material. Explain that, just as adult films have an age guidance rating, there are also websites not suitable for children. If your child comes across unpleasant material, don't make her feel it's her fault. Thank her for telling you.

All that glitters is not gold. Tell children not to be lured by offers or free prizes, or to click on banners that claim they have won things. Tell them that ads and pop-ups are never as good as they look.

FOR OLDER GIRLS:
Switch it off. From early on, turn off your home's broadband connection at a set time every night. Start as soon as they are surfing on their own, and make it non-negotiable. Apart from encouraging the temptation to wander into unsuitable sites, late-night internet use can lead to exhausted, bad-tempered children the next day. However, be aware that older and more determined girls may still try to access the internet on their mobiles. As one mother advised: "I make sure the charger's in the hallway, so they have to plug it in there every night. That way I know she can't take it to bed with her."

Save time with a monitoring service. By the time your daughter's in her early teens, it would be impossible to keep on top of everything she is doing. As soon as your child's social networking is more than you can handle, consider signing up to a service that monitors and sends you alerts when anything sexual, bullying, or drug or alcohol related is posted on any of her networks or communication devices. Some parents resist installing security software because they feel as though they are spying. But in reality it's no worse than the cookies that advertisers save on your computer to track your browsing. Be frank with her about what you are doing so she doesn't feel you are snooping.

Make it a two-way conversation. Telling your daughter "You're on the computer too much" or waiting to catch her on unsuitable websites to tell her off isn't constructive. Instead ask her openly what sites she visited today, and let her know you are going to stay interested. Praise her for showing self-control with her screen time.

Material girls: helping girls fight back against the pressure to buy

Beth's wardrobe is packed full of designer clothes. Her mum, Julie, wants her to have the best, and proudly estimates that she spends several thousand pounds a year so Beth can look stylish in outfits from designer ranges such as Juicy Couture and AppleBottom. Sometimes Beth changes a couple of times before she even turns up at school. At first her friends were impressed. But then another girl in her class told her that her trainers were "all wrong", and some of her friends agreed. So now she's counting down the days until Saturday when she can go to the shops to get the "right ones". Julie really can't afford Beth's new shoes, but she'll get them for her anyway. She knows too well that the right brand names are important to help her daughter fit in.

It's no coincidence that at the same time as our daughters are learning not to like what they see in the mirror, they are also becoming obsessed by consumer brand names. Children start being influenced by marketing as young as eighteen months, when they start recognizing logos. By the age of two, they can even match them with the right products.[57] The issue with aiming products at young people is that they don't have the discrimination to pick and choose. Up to the age of seven children accept everything advertising and marketers tell them without question. And everywhere they go, children are inundated with these messages. There are special TV stations for kids, as well as radio channels and magazines which pump out commercial messages all the time. More marketing messages pop up on mobile phones. Ads appear as banners at the top, sides, and bottoms of websites, or jump out of them uninvited as pop-ups.

After all, kids as consumers are big business. An estimated 350 million pounds was spent in 2009 on advertising to children alone, according to a Mothers' Union investigation into kids and consumerism.[58] In the privacy of their bedrooms, children are sitting targets. Three out of four children between five and sixteen have a television in their rooms. As a result, UK children view between 20,000 and 40,000 television adverts a year.[59] According to Sharon Beder, author of *This Little Kiddy Went to Market: The Corporate Capture of Childhood:* "it is advertising jingles that children sing rather than nursery rhymes".[60] This means that more and more children in today's society think they need "stuff" to fit in. Even when they know full well that advertisements are trying to sell them something, they fall for the messages which imply that without these products they will be "losers".

But of course it still takes a big person to pay. Parents too get caught up in the fear that if they don't get their children the Xbox, Wii, iPod, or iPad, their children will indeed lose out. Because so many activities are based around computers and consoles, parents start to believe that children *have* to have these things in order to play together. When it comes to gadgets, we feel that if we don't buy the latest must-have gadget, our children will be social outcasts. We end up buying our children more and more stuff, just so they can belong. In one US study, 58 per cent of nine- to fourteen-year-olds said they felt the pressure to buy things in order to belong. It's the families least able to afford it who are affected most. Peer pressure has become so acute that one study found that children from poorer homes in the UK said they had no interest in talking to other youngsters who weren't wearing the most fashionable trainers.[61]

So we keep buying to show we care – and to be good parents. A recent survey found that the average teenage bedroom contains £5,257 worth of gadgets, games, and gear. The huge cost includes about £1,700 worth of the latest electrical equipment, £1,000 of clothes, and £250 of trainers.[62] On the poorest council estates, parents end up putting themselves in debt because they don't know how to resist their children's demands for the latest phones and game consoles. After all, how can we say no? Our adult lives are also filled with technology that proves how up to date we are. Consumer culture has become part of how we see ourselves as families.

Of course, to begin with, the consumer world is fun for kids. But the more drawn in they get, the more it leads to unrealistic expectations and disappointment. The more advertisements children see, the more they know what's out there and the more they think they need. And even when they get what they think they want, children don't stay happy. The cycle repeats itself, making them more and more dissatisfied with their lives. As Sue Palmer, author of *Toxic Childhood*, says: "If you get the idea that they are what they own, they are setting themselves up for a life of consumer driven unhappiness."[63]

For girls, the problem can be even more acute because they usually need a wider range of the "right clothes" to fit in with their friendship group. Being fashionable is such a powerful resource that it buys them popularity. And if you don't have the right outfit, the fall-out can be tough. A third of children say not having the right clothes is the third most stressful thing about being a child.[64] Advertising also creates the powerful expectation for girls that there are products out there which can "fix" what they think is wrong with them, or make them more desirable to their peers. Teenagers who hate their hair and want Cheryl Cole's dazzling mane of chestnut curls will find that, despite the glossy pictures, the shampoo she uses won't do the same for them. That's because, if you read the small print, you'll see that Cheryl is wearing expensive hair extensions.

So don't let advertising create a void in your daughter that can never be filled. Teach her how to reject the marketers' messages and that, above all, she is more than the sum of what she owns.

What you can do:

FOR YOUNGER GIRLS:
Don't confuse parental love with possessions. Parents worry deeply that children will lose out if they haven't bought them the latest product. Don't confuse love with indulgence.

Be a good role model. Girls learn consumer habits from their parents. So moderate your own need to buy. Go shopping because you need things, not to cheer yourself up.

Use advertisements as a first step towards media awareness. When teaching girls not to accept everything they see without question, start with ads. Help them realize that commercials are trying to sell them something. They're a great start for teaching media literacy because they're brief and it's easy for kids to understand how biased they are. From there it will be easier to move on to TV, movies, and websites.

Don't buy into brands. Teach girls early that brands are more about perception than reality. Try this experiment. Buy a box of brand name cornflakes and the supermarket own brand version. Ask her to spot the differences in the ingredients. She will find that they are essentially the same product, except the one with the well-known name is substantially more expensive.

Add up the ads. Go through a magazine and play a game of adding up the cost of everything advertised to show them how much they would have to spend if they bought everything they were told to buy.

Don't make shopping your main family activity. For many mothers and daughters, shopping can easily become their main bonding time. Instead find other things to do, such as visiting a museum or art gallery or going for a walk together, to keep you close.

Don't start girls on collecting. Don't encourage an addiction to toys, such as those linked into movie franchises that create endless demands for more accessories. The only winners here will be the manufacturers, who deliberately set out to create constant demand.

Talk about fads and crazes. Uggs, skinny jeans, *High School Musical*: letting fads take hold can be an expensive business, and within a few months you can be left with lots of items your daughter isn't interested in any more. Talk about the crazes which came and went in your childhood – such as Rubik's cubes and pokemon – to show how fleeting trends are.

Play "I spy" with packaging. On a visit to a supermarket recently, I counted fifty different cartoon characters, from Homer Simpson to Dora the Explorer, on food products. Make it a game for kids on your next visit to help make them media savvy about the way food manufacturers try to make them buy.

Watch ad-free TV. Don't leave your daughter in front of a TV churning out a constant stream of advertisements. With younger girls, one of the best ways to avoid them is to stick to non-commercial television, such as CBeebies, for as long as possible, or use DVDs and fast-forward through the commercials.

Use your parent power. Remember that most major companies don't want to be officially censored for being irresponsible towards children. They might be tempted to risk a bit of controversy to get attention, but if they appear irresponsible with the welfare of children, it doesn't look good. Draw attention to things you think are potentially damaging.

Make a complaint. The Advertising Standards Authority is there for a good reason, and all you need to do is fill in a four step email form if you come across something you think takes advantage of children. It can take just one complaint for the ASA to launch an investigation, and for an inappropriate ad to be withdrawn.

FOR OLDER GIRLS:
Point out the small print. As girls get older and worry more about their looks, they are tempted more and more by the allure of

beauty products. Tell them to check the small print to make it clear how fake some of the advertising images are. If your daughter shows an interest in diet aids, tell her to look for escape clauses such as "Only for use as part of a calorie-controlled diet".

Keep talking. Talk to your daughter about where the products we buy come from, how they got here, and issues such as fair trade. Explain there is a human and environmental cost to endless consumerism.

How to unspoil children

It's not just make-up and clothes that makes little girls seem older than they are. An obsession with consumerism can also replace innocence with a grasping precociousness in our daughters. The problem with giving our children everything is that it's never, ever enough. The more you give them the more they want, and the less they will appreciate it. As loving parents, we so often grant their wishes, thinking that it will make them happy, only to find they quickly move on to wanting something else. With the proliferation of new products coming on the market all the time, the demands are potentially never-ending.

Consumerism makes girls prioritize superficial things and distracts them from what's really important. One unpleasant side effect is that parents who thought they were doing the right thing by providing materially for their children find they have ended up with spoiled brats. But even if you realize this has gone too far, it's not too late.

What you can do:

Ask yourself why you are spoiling her. As much as we hate to admit it, part of the reason our daughters crave so much is because we give them too much, without setting any limits. While it's true that marketers are trying to attract them, we are actually paying up. So, first, work out why we feel the need to overindulge our girls. Is it because you work long hours and feel guilty? Are you afraid she won't love you if you say no? Or were you so busy trying to make her life perfect that you forgot to set restrictions? Or maybe you want her to have more than you did as a kid. Work out your own reasons first.

Check that your daughter isn't your status symbol. Are you allowing your daughter to have the latest things as an outward display to your peers that you are a loving – but also an affluent – parent? If so, restrain your spending so that the message that material things are important doesn't rub off on her.

Make her earn it. If you give treats to your daughter all the time, she won't thank you. Instead she'll just take it for granted and want something new the next day. Girls should earn privileges, because they'll automatically respect and appreciate things more when they have to work for them.

Explain how things are going to change. Half-hearted attempts to unspoil children won't be successful. You have to work at it, and make sure your partner is in agreement, as girls are experts at playing their parents off against each other. It's not too late to draw a line. Choose a quiet, neutral time, when your daughter is not asking for anything, to explain to her that money does not come easily and fun things need to be earned. Listen carefully to her questions and try to answer them. You might have to be prepared for a few tantrums, but stick to the rules.

Don't fall for "It's not fair!". Don't let your child pressure you with claims that it isn't fair when you don't buy her what she wants. Noel Janis-Norton of Calmer, Easier, Happier Parenting says: "Children don't really understand the concept of fairness. What they really mean is 'I don't like what you're saying' or 'I thought I'd be getting something you're not going to give me'. Many of our children are among the most privileged in the Western World, so that's not fair either."[65]

Remember that gadgets won't make your daughter cleverer. Many parents shower their children with the latest educational toys, gadgets, and puzzles because they think it will make them cleverer. Yet it won't be the educational apps on your iPad or computer learning games that will make your daughter excel. It will be the amount of time you spend with her, explaining how the world works.

Resist pestering. Parents often buy their children new things because they think they'll get left out at school if they don't have the latest fad. If you really think she might suffer, check it's something you want her to have. Offer her a taster first to see if that satisfies her curiosity. If she's still desperate, tell her she can earn it by doing extra jobs around the house, or by saving up her pocket money.

Drip-feed presents. Many parents know the embarrassment of watching kids opening present after present at birthdays and Christmas, and barely looking up to say thank-you before moving on to the next gift. So, at a quiet time, explain there will be a new rule that gifts will be spaced out throughout the year. Set limits by asking friends and relatives to give just one gift on special occasions – and donating anything else to your child's savings account.

Encourage charity and voluntary work. Teach your daughter that it's not just receiving that makes people feel good. Giving does too. Steer your daughter's priorities away from consumer culture by asking her to help with fundraising for a good cause or by donating toys or clothes to charity – and explaining how it will help others.

Twelve or twenty-two: dressing appropriately for her age

"There is a definite uniform in our group. We all have to have long straight hair and a fringe swept over to one side, short denim skirts, or jeggings and Ugg boots. You'd have to be pretty daring to step outside that."
Abigail, 13

"Whenever I see my thirteen-year-old daughter go out half-dressed in a micro-mini and camisole top, I say: 'It looks like you want to have sex.' When I tell her, she's looks horrified because it's not what she wants. But young girls see so many models and pop stars barely dressed, they just can't see the messages they are sending out by wearing next to nothing. I don't think she really knows why she does it. She just picks up on the idea that it's the right thing to do."
Lucy, mother, 39

At the world's biggest department store, in New York City, thirteen-year-old Lourdes Ciccone is stepping into the spotlight at the launch of her own fashion line, Material Girl. Today she is on the red carpet with her mother, Madonna, answering questions. As her eyes dart nervously around, it's clear that Lourdes has some years to go before she will be as comfortable as her superstar mother in front of the ranks of film crews and photographers. But her outfit today – a micro-mini black dress, ripped black striped tights and high-heeled ankle boots – tells a different story. The ensemble is typical of Lourdes' collection, a mixture of thigh-skimming skirts, transparent lace tops, and bustier corsets in the style that first brought her mother to global attention in the 1980s.

Visit almost any clothes shop on the British high street, and the line between where childhood ends and adulthood begins is already so blurred that it has become indefinable. Clothes are now sold to children with the expectation that they not only feel the need to look pretty, but should also want to look sexy. It may not help that companies such as Next lump three- to sixteen-year-olds together as "older girls" when the appropriate clothes for the two ends of this age spectrum are vastly different.

Abercrombie and Fitch Kids – one of the most highly prized labels for young girls – includes the "cute" and "perfect butt" leggings range. Despite past criticism of their kids' clothing lines, Britain's biggest retailer, Tesco, has marketed T-shirts with the slogans: "Always looking good", "Ooh la la" and "I've got the X Factor".

Try looking for an old-fashioned plain nightdress for an eight-year-old, as I did the other day, and you'll be offered black silky boxer shorts decorated with pink hearts, matched with a skimpy camisole bearing the words "I know I'm so cute". Children are already cute. But giving them these clothes with this message, they are encouraged to think they are only cute because they are showing off certain body parts in a certain way. And while a twenty-five-year-old woman knows what she is doing when she puts on clothes like this, it's not all right to make that decision for a five-year-old.

Of course, most mothers have been amused by the attempts of their young daughters to totter around the house in their high heels. But past a certain age, it's not just dressing up any more. As Linda Papadopoulos points out: "When a little girl feels that being sexy is the reason she is valued, she's more likely to spend time and energy on winning that praise – instead of devoting time to other areas of her life, like education, sport..."[66] If a girl is praised for wearing sexy clothes, she may start to feel that this is what she is valued for. If we buy little girls styles that make them look like grown-ups, there's a risk they will think it's OK to act like grown-ups too.

What you can do:

FOR YOUNGER GIRLS:

Find other ways to make her feel special. While all little girls like to dress up on special occasions such as Hallowe'en and birthdays, try not to make make-up and high heels part of the ritual.

Don't turn children into "Mini-Me"s. Just because miniature versions of what you wear are available in the children's sections on the high street doesn't make it all right to dress your child as you. Little girls have the rest of their lives to wear high heels and camisoles if they choose. Give them space to be children and dress them in clothes they can play freely in.

Avoid designer labels. Why would you devalue your child by making her a walking advertising billboard for a company's products? Young children don't generally know the difference between branded and non-branded clothes, unless you make a big deal of it.

Complain. If you see clothes on the racks that are inappropriate, say so. Write to the shop's head office and ask if they have considered the implications. Shops don't want to look exploitative and irresponsible, and you will also be keeping the issue at the forefront of their minds. Copy the letter to your local newspaper, or email the Mumsnet Let Girls be Girls campaign, which collects a list of inappropriate clothes appearing on the market.[67]

Make your own T-shirts. Buy plain T-shirts and fabric paints and create unique clothes featuring things that are important to your daughter. If she wants to define herself by what she wears, let her make her own statement.

FOR OLDER GIRLS:

Teach her to use a sewing machine. She doesn't have to make anything complicated; even a bandanna or headscarf made out of a fabric she chose herself is a statement of individuality which proves that fashion is about being different. Kids can start using a sewing machine – with help – from the age of about nine.

Agree to compromise. If your daughter has reached a stage when she absolutely refuses to wear the clothes in her wardrobe, don't force her. There are bigger battles. It's probably because she wants to signal her belonging to friendship groups, not because she's showing you a lack of respect. Banning particular clothes will just make them more alluring to her. Try to find a middle way and let her go through a clothing catalogue you both like and give her a budget so you can agree on some outfits. You will feel under less pressure, and there will be fewer rows, than if you go shopping with her.

Ask schools to think twice about "mufti days". Even in primary schools, this can spark a great deal of anxiety among children anxious to wear the right thing. In secondary schools, they can turn into competitions about who wears the shortest skirt, the skimpiest top, and the most make-up. Ask schools to consider fancy dress or themed clothing days instead if they want to make money for charity.

Tell her where fashion comes from. Fashion has become increasingly throw-away, with girls often only wearing cheap items once or twice before claiming they have nothing to wear. Before it gets to that stage, teach your daughter awareness of how cheap clothes are made, and the human cost of sweatshops.

Ask her to think about how other people will view her. By the time your daughter is a teenager, she may have become so desensitized to seeing pop stars walking around in little more than their underwear that she honestly thinks she's fully dressed in next to nothing. If your daughter wants to go out in something that you feel looks provocative, don't scream and shout. If you prohibit her, she'll only sneak the outfit out of the house and put it on at her friend's house. Instead ask her how she thinks she will be perceived. Tell her you understand she wants to look more mature. But explain that while she thinks she looks cool, some people, whose attentions she will not welcome, may think she wants sex. It may not change her mind, but at least you've made her aware of the impression she might create.

Tone it down. If your daughter insists on wearing buttock-skimming shorts and micro minis, suggest she customize them with leggings or camisoles underneath to tone it down. If she is wearing her clothes to look part of her group, rather than to appear sexy, she may not mind provided she still keeps her overall look. Keep explaining that it's not that you don't like her style, but you just want her to keep safe.

Lead by example. It doesn't always follow – the most conservatively dressed mums can sometimes have the most provocatively dressed daughters. But check that you are setting a good example when you go out. Do you parade around the bedroom trying on your sexiest outfits and giving the impression that how you are dressed is your main selling point?

Pretty babies? Drawing the line between make-believe and make-up

"A lot of girls spend break-time applying their make-up in the loos. I find it maddening because the girls are always messing around with lip gloss and powder instead of listening in class too."
Madeleine, secondary school teacher

"I am in Year Four and I don't want to wear make-up but I know there are other girls in my class who want to. They are the group who like Hannah Montana – and they want things like Hannah Montana hair dye and nail polish. I might wear make-up when I am twenty but I am child now and I think children look better without it."
Paulina, 9

"When my daughter came along after my son, I was so excited I couldn't wait to do girly things with her. She was about six when she started to put bits of make-up on, around the same time as I did when I was little. It was fun for me to see her because I wanted a princessy girl. She likes it because she says people notice her more."
Claire, mother, 34

Today six-year-old Rosalie is playing a more sophisticated version of her normal dress-up game. With a sugar pink Alice band in place to pull her hair off her face, she is recording her ten step make-up tutorial for YouTube viewers, inspired by her heroine Hannah Montana. So far 40,000 people have logged on to view her tips. Rosalie clearly knows all the cosmetic lines she uses well. Holding up each product with the expertise of a home shopping channel presenter, she tells how the eye shadow she is using today is in the shade of "Fishnet" from Urban Decay.

Rosalie is far from the only primary school age child on YouTube applying cosmetics like a professional make-up artist. Scroll down the suggested video list on the right of the screen and you will find hundreds of other little girls – some as young as three – doing the same. There is six-year-old Hannah, who also advises fellow "make-up junkies" on how to achieve the "smoky eyed" look. Meanwhile Emma, who is seven, shows off her special Valentine's Day face. For older girls, there are also plenty of routines to perfect the "back to school" look.

While viewers tell them, "You're so cute," seeing small children applying full foundation on flawless skin and chubby cheeks is actually rather poignant. They are already infected by the notion that, however beautiful they are, it's not enough. But, of course, a growing market in products and services is encouraging little girls to think that way. Up and down the country, spas offer them makeovers and manicures. A company called Giddy Diva Pamper Parties offers children as young as four "a dazzling selection of make-up and glitter" for their special day. Another company proudly boasts: "No more pin the tail on the donkey. Look out, your daughters will be blown away from mini-manicures to hair glitter right in the comforts of their own homes!"

It's a mini beauty industry that's also being fostered by the recent craze for high school proms, sparked by the *High School Musical* films. At these events, even primary school age girls get prepped and pampered all day by beauticians, who do their hair and nails ready for the moment when they pose, celeb-like, in Barbie-style gowns next to limos.

As Adele Wilk, proud mum of seven-year-old Ellie, gushed after the prom at Maerdy infant school in Rhondda, South Wales: "She looked so grown up, like a little adult, and even had flowers round her wrist. She wore make-up including lip gloss, and she was so thrilled. We hired a limousine for her and eight friends, which cost £12 each, and the limo took them round the village before dropping them at school." So widespread is the trend, that prom companies now tour the country's schools, handing out flyers for local beauty treatments, including hair extensions and spray-on tans.[68]

But, of course, there's no need to wait for a special occasion. The opportunities for beautification start in the aisles of Britain's biggest toy chain, Toys "R" Us, where girls of any age can get their parents to buy them a "Dream Dazzler Light Up Glamour Make-up" set for £14.99 or a "Who Do You Adore?" make-up set for £19.99. For their older sisters, major make-up brands, such as Murad and Bobbi Brown, are bringing out product lines especially for young girls.

The cosmetics industry is, of course, thrilled by the emergence of a previously untapped market. As one of its own news websites, Fashion Industry Today, reports: "Younger girls desire to wear make up at such a young age in an attempt to express their independence and to also be more like their popular idols – women such as Lindsay Lohan, Hillary Duff, and Miley Cyrus. Girls just want to be part of the in crowd." As they also point out: "Marketing agencies are well aware of this and have stepped up to the plate creating and manufacturing products that are specifically designed for young girls between the ages of 9 and 12. It's a marketing haven."[69] With so much encouragement, it's no surprise that a recent report found that use of make-up among tweens up to the age of twelve has doubled since 2007.[70]

Of course, what mother has not caught her little girl at her dressing table, daubing on rouge? But with parents of girls as young as eight telling me their girls routinely wear lip gloss, rouge and mascara, the risk is that by starting them early, our daughters believe their time and energy should mostly be spent improving their looks.

If a little girl spends her time looking in the mirror searching for flaws to fix, it doesn't take long for her to think that a face without make-up isn't good enough. Too early, she will be set on a life-long path of dissatisfaction that no cosmetic can ever cure.

What starts as lipstick and mascara for a special occasion can quickly develop into a can't-do-without. One mother told me that, by the age of twelve, her daughter never left the house without spending forty minutes putting on her make-up in the bathroom. "The saddest thing is she comes out looking worse – because there's nothing really to improve on – but without it she feels she can't face the world." It's true that make-up may make our girls temporarily feel good about themselves, but only because they are made to feel they are not good enough in the first place. What's more, far from making them stand out, the irony is that our daughters can all get the same extensions for the same shiny, straight hair, use the same self-tanners to dye their skin the same colour, and wear the same identical false lashes for the same long-lashed look. If you observe groups of teenage girls hanging out together, you will see far from standing out, they look like clones.

It's a tough one to argue for many mums because grown women can be improved by make-up in a way that children aren't. But little girls don't need makeovers because there's nothing wrong with them in the first place. It may be difficult for mothers who use make-up themselves to argue about this, but, for as long as possible, let's concentrate on encouraging our girls to be unselfconscious, to play freely with things that don't centre on looks, rather than worrying if their mascara is running or their lipstick has smudged.

What you can do:

FOR YOUNGER GIRLS:

Don't exaggerate the importance of "prettiness". Yes, girls need to be told they are beautiful, or they will assume they aren't. But make it just one part of who she is, and acknowledge her strength, skills, intelligence, and personality too.

Divert her attention from make-up into crafts. There's no denying that girls are interested in adornment, so channel her creativity for as long as possible into craft kits to make jewellery. She will probably spend more time making it than wearing it.

Avoid handing cosmetics out in party bags and as presents. I have lost count of the number of party bags my children have come home with containing lipsticks and nail varnishes. Even if you don't mind it for your own daughter, spare other mothers the battle.

Explain your reasons early. At some point, your daughter will be invited to a playdate or a party where other little girls put on make-up. Explain early on to your daughter that while this may be what some of her friends do, your family has different values. Take the time to explain what yours are – and why they are in place to protect her.

Focus on the present. Try not to fast-forward by speculating on how attractive your daughter will look as a full-grown woman. Instead focus on the here and now of her childhood.

FOR OLDER GIRLS:
Don't scold. Acknowledge that she may insist on wearing make-up because she feels she needs to fit in or is worried about not being able to get a boyfriend. Tell her you understand she wants to look attractive. But ask her to question if it's also distracting her from other things, such as sport and school work.

Teach her that make-up is to protect her looks. Divert her from lipstick to lip balm, and from foundation to tinted moisturiser with an SPF, to send her the message that the best make-up protects and enhances, rather than covers and masks.

Don't let her see make-up as a quick fix. At neutral times, when you are not fighting over the issue, explain that real beauty comes from healthy, fresh-faced looks, best achieved by eating a balanced diet, drinking enough water, and sleeping well. Everyone has unique features that they can accentuate with make-up, but stress that cosmetics don't make you who you are.

Show her that make-up isn't always attractive. Show examples of celebrities who look worse plastered with cosmetics, and point out that boys are often frightened and put off by "war paint".

Put things in perspective. Teach her how standards of beauty have changed through the ages – and why. Tell her that women used to use lead to give themselves white skin and wore corsets to shrink their waists to 18 inches. Show her how social pressures have made women conform to looking a certain way, even when it was uncomfortable – and bad for their health.

Don't be too preoccupied with make-up yourself. Avoid making comments about how you can't be "seen dead" without your "face on". Don't run for cover if someone tries to take your picture when you're not fully made up. Send the message that you wear make-up primarily to protect and enhance, not to make you look like someone you are not.

Set good examples. Admire other women who don't wear make-up, and show your girls you are happy to leave the house without a fully made-up face and still hold your head up high.

Limit exposure to appearance-obsessed TV programmes. A large part of the appeal of shows such as *Gossip Girl* is that they provide an endless stream of new make-up and hair styles. Don't encourage your daughter in that direction, and if necessary point out how many hours of time, effort, and expertise from make-up artists it will have taken to achieve those looks.

Let her experiment if she insists. Understand that your daughter might want to experiment, but emphasize she is still lovely without make-up. Show her old pictures of herself growing up to illustrate that she looked beautiful before and will look beautiful again if she chooses not to wear it.

Guide her safely. Some guidance on how to apply make-up can also be a good idea if she insists on wearing it. Teenagers often assume they need more than they really do. If she's often making herself look worse rather than better, consider getting her some advice at a cosmetics counter. She may feel the need to wear less if she's more confident about how to apply it.

Give her the commercial realities. Discuss issues such as testing on animals and the fact that there are health doubts about chemicals in make-up. Point out that, by weight, make-up is one of the most expensive commodities in the world.

Ask for the school's policy on make-up. This may not stop your daughter adding a slick of lip gloss on the bus on the way to school, but it will keep other parents conscious of the issue, and at least foster an atmosphere in which make-up is not encouraged.

Finding good role models

"As a teacher, I have come across girls in my class who look at Colleen Rooney and have said, 'Oh, I'd just love her lifestyle' – and they really mean it. When I've had to talk to other girls about their work, I've also heard: 'Don't worry, Miss. I can marry a footballer' – and they're only half joking. Seeing people become famous through no talent has definitely contributed to a something for nothing culture in schools. Some kids think they don't have to work as hard because somehow they'll find a way to get it all to land in their laps."

Louise, teacher, 29

"When I started writing an agony aunt column fifteen years ago, I would get letters from girls asking how to be doctors and scientists. Now I'm getting letters from girls who say they want to be famous, but don't know how because there's nothing they're good at."

Hilary Freeman, agony aunt

Considering the advances that women have made within society over the last two generations, it's telling that 42 per cent of girls name celebrities as their greatest influences: Victoria Beckham, Cheryl Cole, Katie Price, Colleen Rooney, Selina Gomez, Paris Hilton, and most recently Kate Middleton. Boys admire sports stars, but the women that girls look up to are chiefly worshipped for being size 10 or less, or envied for their spending power or who they are married to. Sportswomen, business leaders, or politicians are rarely mentioned.

The messages that girls take away from these examples are many and varied. While most girls admire the fact that these women look in control, they also conclude that who you marry or date will enhance your wealth and status, and that thin means successful. The fact that the acronym WAG for "Wives and Girlfriends" even exists shows how much status women are seen to get from being attached to a rich and powerful male. New celebrities are also elevated from obscurity by reality TV shows, so it is unsurprising that girls can come to believe that wealth and fame can be achieved overnight, either by meeting the right man or by going on TV. Seven out of ten teachers now believe that celebrity culture is perverting children's aspirations and encouraging a generation to believe that you can be successful without hard work.

A girl's first female role model should be her mother. But, beyond that, we are not fulfilling our role as parents if we do not encourage our girls to raise their eyes higher – to women who are known for their determination, hard work, and strength.

What you can do:

Ask her what she admires about her role model. If your daughter attaches herself to a female role model, make sure she doesn't just worship her blindly. Encourage a balanced view by asking what characteristics are really important, and help her to see the bigger picture.

Don't hero worship. As a parent, worshipping celebrities belittles you and gives famous people more importance than they deserve. No one's superhuman. Don't make your child feel any less special than the people she sees on TV and in magazines.

Make your own role models close to home. Help girls look beyond the cult of youth and celebrity, and praise the people that you know personally for kindness and generosity.

Find inspiration in today's real role models. Log on to www.pinkstinks.co.uk for a Real Role Model of the Month. These are women from all backgrounds and walks of life who will show your daughter that she can be whatever she wants to be.

Make-up and spots

One important reason that many girls become reliant on make-up is because they develop spots during puberty. At this particularly sensitive time, when they are trying so hard to present a "pretty face" to the world, and when acceptance is partly dictated by looks, it's no exaggeration to say that acne can have a catastrophic effect on their self-esteem. The feelings of despair, hopelessness, and mortifying self-consciousness can affect even the most confident girl. Girls can become isolated and depressed, and unable to look in the mirror in the mornings, leading to feelings of self-hatred and shame. Covering spots leads to a slippery slope of more make-up use, because the more cover-up and foundation they have to apply, the more it has to be balanced with lip and eye make-up.

Yet while as many as 85 per cent of twelve- to twenty-five-year-olds suffer from spots, only 15 per cent seek medical treatment for their condition, even though treatments have come a long way in the last few years and in Britain the NHS takes the condition far more seriously than it used to. So even if you think she's making too much of a fuss about a few pimples, listen to her concerns, and if the spots persist, think about getting help. At this time of her life, your daughter really needs to be able to turn her face to the light.

"When I grow up I want to be thin": helping girls fight back

"My daughter is 5ft 7ins tall with a lovely face and beautiful body because she is very keen on sport. You'd think there'd be nothing anyone could pick on, but one day she came home saying she was ugly. When I got to the bottom of it, one of the girls had picked on the fact that one tooth was slightly longer than the other. You'd have thought her world had caved in."
Alison, mother, 41

"How much we all weigh is one of our main topics of conversation. No one's ever happy with their own weight. We all take turns complaining about our bodies and saying which celebrity's bottom or boobs we'd like. Then we like to find out what diets they are trying and give them a try. We are always trying to take thin pictures of ourselves to put on Facebook. It's important to have a really good profile picture to get more friends."
Joanna, 14

"I have struggled with my weight all my life – and I had tried to hide it from my daughter. But the message still got through to her. She's lovely but I see her looking in the mirror and pulling her appearance apart. Then one day as I was getting ready to go out she said to me, 'You know, you are much prettier than you think you are.' It broke my heart because I realized my poor self-image about my looks had rubbed off on her."
Niki, mother, 35

Children begin to recognize themselves in the mirror at about two years old. It is a sobering thought that within just a few years little girls – but, interestingly, not little boys – who are barely old enough to write the alphabet already look back at their reflections and don't like what they see. Half of three- to six-year-old girls say they worry about being fat, according to research published in the *British Journal of Developmental Psychology*. By the time the girls are aged between eleven and seventeen, being thin is their number one wish in life. Instead of seeing their true reflections, girls become trapped in a maze of fairground mirrors, with a distorted idea of what it is to be normal.[71]

So, how do even young children so quickly get the message that in this society thin is perfect, fat means failure, and a person's worth drops in inverse proportion to their weight? Painful though it may be to admit, the first lessons girls get about their bodies come from home, from us. Low calorie, low fat, high carb, low protein, gluten-free... Considering that food is such a simple and essential commodity, we've made it incredibly complicated. As I found with my own daughter, the word "diet" doesn't even have to be mentioned in the home for the message to filter through.

As they observe us skipping meals, getting on the scales, obsessing about weight, and criticizing our bodies, girls quickly realize that food is very powerful, with the ability to make their parents feel guilty and depressed. Food is always, always on our minds. Within, most women wage an ongoing war to achieve or keep their ideal weight, dominated by nagging voices asking: "Is it OK to eat this?", "How fat do I look today?" and "Have I eaten too much?" For those who live in a society where food is plentiful and cheap, thinness can be seen as a measure of self-control and worth. A recent experiment found that the average adult woman has a negative thought about her body and appearance thirty-six times a day, so it's hardly surprising our daughters pick up on this preoccupation, whether we try to hide it or not.[72]

Even conscientious mums who try actively to be examples of healthy living, and never ask: "Does my bum look big in this?", can end up sending out unbalanced messages that their girls pick up on. As Deanne Jade, founder of the National Centre for Eating Disorders, says: "Even if you think you are modelling good behaviour by telling your daughter you are going to the gym to get healthy, not thin, it can create the anxiety in a child that it's the only way to be healthy... Everything we say sends a message which can be much louder to the ears of a child. Leading a healthy lifestyle is not about modelling our own perfectionist standards. It's about modelling a balanced sense of self-care."[73]

It's a difficult fact to face up to. But as our child's first and biggest influence, we have to look to ourselves. Today's mothers grew up in the 1960s, 1970s, and 1980s, when stick-thin proportions were admired more and more. Now we have children ourselves, consciously or unconsciously we pass this ideal along to our daughters. Moreover, as soon as a girl who has learned these messages from her mother steps into the outside world, she finds them reinforced even further. In our children's eyes, we are proved right when every time they open a magazine or switch on a TV, the only glamorous and successful women they see are size 10 or less. With all this swirling around our children, it's hardly surprising that the most feared insult among them is the word "fat". So, when it comes to body image, we have to fight the battle on two fronts: against our own hang-ups and against the messages that bombard our daughters constantly from everywhere else.

What you can do:

FOR YOUNGER GIRLS:

When it comes to diet, the most important thing is what we don't say. Stop making food an ongoing topic of conversation in your household. Even if you think you are spreading healthy eating messages, you are making food a big issue. Instead, without a fuss or fanfare, quietly make sure a good range of nutritious good food is available in your home. Keep in mind that there are no "bad" foods. What is bad is when we don't eat them in a balanced way. The best thing you can do for your daughter is to make eating normally no big deal, just a part of life.

Never mention the word "diet". Overhearing your endless conversations with your friends about the latest diet regime can make girls think it's a woman's lot to starve herself. If dieting is mentioned by other adults in front of your daughter, quickly and quietly change the subject.

Get girls involved in cooking. Get them back in touch with food, where it comes from, and how it is made. Make meal-times a stress-free family occasion by focusing on companionship and conversation, not who's eating what.

Encourage a wide variety of exercise. Make a broad range of different physical activities a natural and normal part of life – whether it's skating, swimming, or going for a walk in the park.

Trust that your daughter knows when she's hungry and when she's full. Professor of Obesity, Julia Buckroyd, says: "Listen to your children when they say they've had enough. Don't push for them to finish everything on their plate. Parents too often try and force food on children. It can destroy the natural internal mechanisms that control our intake. Young children are pretty good at knowing when they are satisfied."[74]

Check that dads know not to make remarks. Criticisms made by a father about his daughter's – or indeed any woman's – weight can cut particularly deep, because she will assume that's how all men think. Ask your partner to check his own attitudes.

Watch your child's posture. If your daughter suddenly goes from standing up straight to slouching and hiding, she may be going through painful feelings about her body image that you may be able to help her with.

Don't express regret or guilt over food. How many of us have groaned after dinner, "I wish I hadn't eaten that"? Don't talk about "fat days". Stop sending the message that food is something to feel guilty about.

Don't reward your daughter with food. Look for other ways to say "well done", such as trips, books, and special times together.

Compliment your child's body on what it does – not what it looks like. Find a sport your daughter loves, so she sees her body as something useful and powerful, not something to be judged on appearance alone. Praise her for the skilful way she plays tennis or does gymnastics. Praise female athletes for their strength and skills and their muscle tone instead of admiring celebrities for their skinny figures.

Give up control. Ultimately it will be up to your daughter what she eats, so give up commenting and criticizing. Don't insist she finishes off her food or monitor her junk food intake, or she will start to eat in secret. It's more important that you maintain a good overall relationship with her and set a good example.

FOR OLDER GIRLS:
With care, diet may never become an issue. But if it does, you will need to tread very carefully to counteract any negative ideas your daughter may have formed.

If overeating is becoming a problem, get to the root. First check your own attitudes. Is she really getting overweight, or is she simply not conforming to your mental template of how you would like her to look? Remember, too, that it's normal for girls to put on 20 per cent of body weight in fat during puberty. But if you are certain your child has put on weight to the point of obesity, and you are afraid it will lead to teasing and self-esteem problems, then look at possible emotional causes. Professor Julia Buckroyd says: "Ask yourself: 'Is this child unhappy – or bored?

What's going on at school?' For children nowadays there are very few ways of registering distress except for bad behaviour and overeating."[75]

Prepare her for starting her periods. It can be deeply worrying for a girl to be on tenterhooks about when her period will start, or what would happen if it surprised her in the middle of a lesson, and the humiliation that would result. Log on to pogopack.co.uk for advice about how she can prepare herself and reduce the worry.

Ask her what pressures she feels under. If a child starts obsessing about weight, it's often because she's worried about something else. Eating disorders expert Deanne Jade says: "If my child told me she's fat, I wouldn't answer. I'd say: 'What's worrying you? Come over here for a hug.' Ask her to write down her worries about body image, so she can see them in black and white. By externalizing, she may be better able to see the pressures on her more clearly."[76]

Pick your moments. At neutral times, not at a time when your girl is insecure about her looks, explain that what makes someone an attractive person to be around is the sum of all their parts – not just one. Praise other women for their strength and personality.

Teach children media awareness. Explain that not even models and celebrities look like the images we see in the media, thanks to airbrushing and stylists.

Never refer to your daughter's shape except to reject a negative comment. If she expresses reservations about the way she looks, listen carefully, without dismissing her worries initially. Don't agree, or say "You're fine". Suggest that we often judge ourselves more harshly than we need to, and ask her if she thinks she might be being overly critical. Remind her that she wouldn't allow anyone else to say things like that to her, so why should she say it to herself? Explain that even the most famously beautiful women in the world are never completely satisfied – and as soon as one flaw is "fixed", another comes to the fore. Tell her obsessing over looks is not only pointless, but that it also leads to unhappiness.

Listen to her. Eating disorders are often the last resort for girls who are not being heard any other way, says Julia Buckroyd. Doing too much and under pressure to be perfect, they don't have a voice, so they protest using things they do have control over: food or self-harm. Make sure your children can really talk to you – and you hear what they are really saying, not what you want to hear.

Talk about different body types. Self-acceptance is a key part of developing a healthy body image. Talk about the fact that there are different body types that are laid down in our genes; models just have the DNA that makes them tall and thin. Explain that a healthy weight is different for every woman, based on her build and height.

Explain differences in development. Your daughter may go into a panic if she feels she is developing too soon or too slowly. Have a conversation early on and explain that people go through puberty at different times, and that things such as breast development and periods can happen at different times to different girls.

Define a new type of beauty. Create your own ideas of beauty by admiring other women outside the stereotype. Don't labour the point but talk about how the best way to care for ourselves is a balance of good food, sleep, and being active in lots of different ways.

Explain the concept of being too thin. Tell her that being thin and undernourished is no more healthy or attractive than being obese, and though boys may claim to like very slim girls, in reality it's more likely they prefer normal, more natural shapes.

Don't judge others on what they look like. If you're constantly commenting on what other women look like, then your daughter will start to rate herself by the same standards. When you talk about other people, talk about their positive personal qualities instead, such as loyalty and kindness.

Emphasize bearing. Tell her how grace, bearing, and posture are the best ways to show off her poise and figure.

Branded: resisting fashion and beauty advertising

"Whenever I open a magazine, I feel fatter, uglier, and more depressed. But at the same time, I can't stop myself picking them up."
Miriam, 16

The other day I counted all the images of women my elder daughter saw on her way home from school on the bus: in her half-hour journey I added up more than twenty. Most were of women, partially dressed or presented in underwear: in general they wore 20 to 50 per cent less clothing than the men. Some were repeated several times over. When I took a fresh look around me, I was not surprised that my younger daughter Clio, who is five, recently asked me: "Why do people thinks boobs are so important?"

It's nothing new that the female body is being used as a way to sell things. But whereas once billboards were full of stereotypical domesticated women, now they are dominated by a stereotype of a different kind. She is the semi-dressed, sexually aggressive, provocative babe. She has leapt from the pages of soft porn, which has been nudged into the mainstream by the hard-core variety. Everywhere we look, the commercial message of these images works on our anxieties, exposing or creating vulnerabilities and telling grown-up women that they need to be younger, smoother, and firmer. Advertising works by making us feel we are missing something. If it works on us as adult women, how much more powerful and damaging must it be to young girls who are still looking to find their place in the world? How does it affect those who aren't old enough to know that no product will magically make them into the person they are told they should be?

Try spending a day looking at these messages through the eyes of a child who is still trying to form an idea of what it is to be female. By the time girls are teenagers, they start to seek out these images more actively in the pages of magazines, which they read to try and work out how they are supposed to look. As one girl surveyed by Girlguiding UK explained: "When I was eleven, I read a teenage magazine for the first time and that is when it kind of clicked: 'I should be like this.'"[77] But, of course, no one can be. Studies consistently find that the women on TV and in magazines are on average 15 per cent thinner than normal, and the great majority of magazine pictures have now been digitally perfected. Yet girls still take these images to heart. A 2005 study of nearly 140 British girls aged eleven to sixteen found that exposure to images of magazine models drastically lowered the girls' body satisfaction and self-esteem.[78]

As a teenager in the 1980s, even before the explosion of magazines aimed at this age group, I had a scrapbook. When I found a picture of a model I liked I would cut her out and paste her in. It was a peculiar form of self-torture. I would spend hours trying to work out how these girls looked so perfect, when I saw no such flawless beauties in the real world. I was still growing; my skin was in turmoil; and my features were not yet in proportion. And, to this day, I still remember the pain of feeling that I was never going to measure up to those girls with perfect skins and delicate noses.

That was thirty years ago. So imagine how our daughters feel today, with such images multiplied a thousand times over in magazines deliberately aimed at them, telling them they can look like celebrities. On average, our daughters see 400 images a day to show them what it means to be beautiful. It starts with magazines targeting young girls, such as *Barbie* magazine and *Disney Girl*. But as soon as our girls have finished with ponies and fairies, they are presented with tips on make-up and boys. An analysis of young girls' magazines by the Australia Institute found up to 75 per cent of their content was sexualizing material.[79]

What you can do:

Limit your child's exposure to beauty and fashion magazines. Magazines carry more advertisements for beauty products than they do articles. You may have learned how to filter these messages out but young girls haven't. There are lots of other interesting publications you can leave around the house. For tweens, offer them alternatives such as *New Moon*. It contains no ads and is edited by girls, aged eight and up, themselves.

Discuss the fine line between inappropriate and fashionable. If she's obsessed with celebrities, show her beautifully dressed women who don't have to show off too much flesh.

Read magazines together. If she's interested in fashion, by all means look at the latest editions, but talk about how unreaslistic the pictures are.

Complain. If you see an article in a magazine aimed at girls that you think is sexually irresponsible then you can complain to the Teenage Magazine Arbitration Panel – the industry's self-regulatory body, which is supposed to ensure that "the sexual content of teenage magazines is presented in a responsible and appropriate manner". If we don't complain, there's a risk the magazine industry will maintain there's no problem.

Teaching your daughter the F-word

I can still remember when, as a five-year-old, watching the Miss World contest was one of the TV highlights of my year. Because no one had told me anything different, when I saw the pretty ladies up on stage modelling swimsuits and crowned with tiaras, I thought that must be the pinnacle of achievement for a woman. I clearly remember telling my father: "I want to be Miss World when I grow up." But as I did grow, I also became aware of the demonstrations that surrounded the event. Seeing others protesting opened my eyes up to the fact that women should not be judged and given marks out of ten like livestock. As a result, I changed my mind about what I wanted to be – and hoped for more for myself.

Thanks to such protests, women did get more rights in the workplace, and it started to look as if the battle had been won. Then the media and pop culture struck back. Madonna's conical bras started to make sexual posing seem empowering to women; "girl power" helped make it acceptable for women to be sexually aggressive; and pornography became chic and daring for them. Despite how far it had brought them, feminism became a dirty word for many women, because they didn't want to be seen as humourless man-haters. We have ended up sleepwalking into a society where "sexual liberation" has made our daughters think that they have to be slutty to be sexy and that confidence means taking your clothes off.

In a straw poll of teenage girls, I found that most didn't have a clue what feminism was – or that women had even needed it. But without it, how do our daughters know that their gender has a voice, that things can change, and that they don't have to fit into today's empty stereotypes if they don't want to? So, as your daughter gets older, tell her how hard women have had to fight until relatively recently. Get her to keep questioning whether there is gender equality, not just in the workplace but in how people are expected to look and behave. Otherwise our daughters won't know how far they have come – or how far they still need to go.

Channelling sex: how exposure to TV affects girls and what to do about it

Look back once more to your own childhood, and you may find that some of your most vivid memories are of the programmes you saw on television. The other day I surprised myself by singing my elder daughter the theme tune to *Top Cat*, a cartoon I had not seen in maybe thirty-five years. Along the way, television left me with other deep impressions. Even now, I can still see myself hiding behind the sofa as the Daleks took to the streets on *Dr Who*.

Television strongly affected me, even though I probably had much less access to it than the youngsters of today. Now TVs have become so cheap and plentiful that virtually every member of the family has a set of their own. There are pink TVs designed just for girls to have in their bedrooms. Nearly 60 per cent of five- and six-year-olds already have their own TVs, and nearly nine out of ten teenagers.

Furthermore, where once there was a watershed, now children can watch anything at any time thanks to cable, pay-per-view, and internet on-demand TV, which means they can encounter unsuitable programming at any time of the day or night.

All this begs the question: "What memories of television will our children grow up with?" We don't know how it will affect them, since we don't know what they are seeing, and we are not there to watch it with them. The problem is that children are not ready to choose to reject what TV tells them. Just like the images in fashion magazines, they think it's real – and most of the time we are not there to tell them it is not. As one eleven-year-old girl told me about school drama *Waterloo Road*: "It's all the same things that happen at our school – just they happen every day there."

Children spend more time watching television than in any other activity except sleep, so it's not surprising that it can have a big impact. There is no longer a debate about whether children mimic behaviour they have seen on television. Over 1,000 studies have found a link between media violence and aggressive behaviour in children. Kids who watched violent shows were found to be more likely to strike out at other children, row, and disobey authority, and were less willing to wait for things than children who viewed programmes without violence.[80] Cumulative violence can lead children to form a view of the world as a dangerous, threatening place. Likewise, a constant stream of programmes featuring sex can make it into their main preoccupation.

As parental concern has increasingly turned towards the internet, the spotlight has moved away from TV, which parents now view as relatively safe compare, to the unknown other world that is the web. We quickly assume that many TV shows must be suitable for our children because they are on before 9.00 p.m. Take *Hannah Montana*, a programme that many parents allow girls as young as three or four to watch. It's the story of the adventures of a tween transformed into a pop star by blonde highlights and make-up. She claims to be thirteen, but acts twenty-five. YouTube is full of videos of little girls sharing "Hannah Montana make-up tips". Other young fans compete to show how much merchandise they own from the show, from pillows and lunch-boxes to face masks, lip glosses, eye shadows, and body lotions. At my daughter's school, by Year Four clear social divisions have started to form along the lines of which TV programmes and films girls watch. My daughter tells me that the girls who watch Hannah Montana have broken away to talk about make-up and hairstyles, the Harry Potter fans role-play about wizards, while the rest, who are not hooked on any TV programmes or movies, play with skipping ropes and ponies.

A starker illustration of the power of TV is the experience of Fiji, where, before TV was introduced, women were admired for having full, curvy figures. Researchers at Harvard Medical School found that body dissatisfaction among girls rose from 12.7 per cent to 29.2 per cent within three years of the arrival of TV.

Dieting among teenagers who watched TV also soared to two in every three girls. As the psychologist Dr Aric Sigman points out: "An abundance of skinny women on-screen makes viewers question their own attractiveness or 'mating value'. Not to be left behind, women compete losing weight themselves. Modern life has hijacked an ancient survival mechanism."[81]

If anything, TV has just as much of an effect on our children as the internet, because the constant sex is dressed up as real in dramas, instead of being live action porn. A study of 1,792 adolescents aged between twelve and seventeen found that children with higher exposure to sex on TV were almost twice as likely than children with lower exposure to start having sex.[82]

Children themselves are aware that television affects the way they behave. Again, tellingly, it's the generation who have just left their teenage years behind who disapprove most of young kids viewing TV that is too old for them. According to a BBC poll of more than 1,000 people, a surprising 78 per cent of eighteen- to twenty-four-year-olds believe that tougher restrictions are needed to help put teenagers off having sex so soon.[83]

But the influence of television goes beyond traditional concerns about "sex and violence". Competitive programmes about makeovers and weight loss create a distorted, bitchy view of life for girls. Most of the viewers of shows such as *Big Brother*, *I'm a Celebrity*, and *Britain's Next Top Model* are under the age of twenty-four. Programmes such as these create a world of throw-away friendships, rejection, exclusion, and back-stabbing, where personal criticism and bullying are encouraged and everyone is divided into winners and losers. Beauty and sex appeal are portrayed as ways to win friends and manipulate people.

Don't trust the people who make these programmes to be thinking of your child's emotional well-being, when they know that pushing the boundaries wins ratings. When the Parents' TV Council in the US branded *Gossip Girl* as "mind-blowingly inappropriate", the show revelled in the description, using the phrase above a shot of a naked teenage couple in bed to advertise the next series. You would not let someone who behaved as people do on TV through your front door – so why allow them in via an electronic box in your children's bedrooms?

What you can do:

Be age appropriate. Just because they're too old for CBeebies doesn't mean they're ready for everything else shown before the watershed. Six-year-olds certainly shouldn't be parked in front of soap opera. Make sure the programmes they are watching are right for their age.

Watch TV with your daughter. Parents can transform TV into a learning tool by watching with their children rather than just dumping them in front of the screen. Use what you see as a starting point for talking about difficult issues.

Understand what she's watching. As she gets older, tune in to the programmes she wants to watch for at least a couple of episodes, or if you are short of time check out extracts on YouTube. If you know what she's watching, you'll be able to see what messages she is taking away and discuss them. Keep putting what she sees in context.

Add up her screen time. When you add TV to internet use and video-game time, the average British child is spending five hours and eighteen minutes in front of a screen each day – more time than they spend in the classroom.[84] Don't allow your daughter to slump in front of the TV and then surf the net for hours. Come up with a daily limit for screen time in total, and ask her to choose between the TV and the computer. Don't allow both.

Don't let TV baby sit your daughter. Parents feel more in control letting kids watch TV because it's more regulated than the web. That doesn't make it a responsible babysitter. If your daughter has developed a glassy-eyed, zombie look as she watches, it's time to wake her out of her trance.

Don't make TV a fact of life. If it's not too late, you may find you are better off not letting your daughter watch broadcast television at all. Instead limit her viewing to DVDs and programmes you pre-record or download. It may not last forever but you will have preserved a few more years of her girlhood.

Don't abandon her to commercial TV. Advertisements just create a desire for things that kids never even knew existed. If she doesn't know commercial TV exists, don't show it to her.

Complain. Put the image of Mary Whitehouse out of your mind forever. Would it really be so bad if you stood up and voiced your concern? Write to Ofcom if you think programmes are damaging to your daughter.

Understand TV classification. Learn how the systems on different channels work – and stick to them. Point them out to your daughter to show it's not just you who is concerned about what's safe for her to watch. Consider TV controls that screen out unsuitable material.

Don't allow TV into the bedroom. The best way of keeping television out of the bedroom is never to let it in there in the first place. Make it a rule that no one has a TV in their room. Keep the TV firmly in the living room where viewing is a family activity. Make television a collective, shared experience by holding family movie nights.

Plan ahead. Go through the TV guides once a week and agree how your daughter is going to spend her screen time. Work with her to establish rules about how much TV she uses.

Never leave the TV on in the background. Even if it's just music videos or news, this is a bad precedent. Make TV a privilege, not a right that is always available day or night.

Consider dropping cable or satellite TV. Unless you're an obsessive sports fan, do you really need the extra channels, which are even harder to keep track of? If you do, use the parental controls.

The pornification of pop: the messages in music videos and how to deal with them

It's 4.30 p.m. We've just got home from school and I can hear my then four-year-old daughter Clio rehearsing a new song she's just learned at her school dance club in front of the full-length mirror in the living room. At first, the words all melt into one. But, gradually, I can pick Clio's own half-remembered version of the song: "I'm a single ladee, I am a single ladee… I've got a man on my hips and lipstick on my lips." While the full implication of the words may be lost on her, it's clear from the way Clio is wiggling her bottom, in a tentative version of Beyoncé's booty-shaking *tour de force*, that she thinks she looks grown up. And from the gratified way she looks in the mirror, I can tell she likes what she sees.

Clio was doing what many little girls do for recreation these days. Look on YouTube and you will see hundreds of films of toddlers and young girls miming explicit lyrics and sexy dance moves to Lady Gaga, Beyoncé, and Britney songs. When my older daughter Lily, then eight, sang at a charity fund-raiser in the Albert Hall, one of the numbers she was asked to sing was "Bad Romance" by Lady Gaga. But then it's hardly surprising when these songs are already the soundtrack to their school discos and birthday parties. Despite calls for a 9.00 p.m. watershed, there are currently no limits at all on pop videos, however explicit the images or the messages – these videos are pumped out day and night on twenty-four hour music channels. Because it's all set to a beat, the lyrics all too often slip under the radar of parents until they hear their children coming out with lines about riding on a "disco stick".

Again, many parents may not have noticed how much music videos have changed. When I was growing up, the sight of the two female singers from Abba in blue satin jump-suits blowing kisses through dry ice was as raunchy as it got. These days in music videos, if you're a woman wearing anything more than a bra, pants and suspenders, or buttock skimming shorts, you are seriously overdressed. If women do wear clothes, they are fetish chic – sky-high platforms, thigh high boots and corsets. No one better exemplifies the move from soft porn to music than the Pussycat Dolls. Originally formed as a burlesque dance group of strippers, their manager secured them a record deal on the strength of their raunchy appeal and sexually provocative songs like "Don't Cha", in which the girls taunt a man by saying he must wish his girlfriend was "as hot" as they are. The group's philosophy revolves around the idea that what is most important is being "sexy" and being an object of lust from men, and envy from other women.

Nor will girls find positive role models in more established female solo artists like Katy Perry, who is currently dominating the charts. Despite her song-writing talents, Katy can't seem to resist pushing the boundaries of child-like, innocent imagery like dolls, sweets, and lollipops to the absolute limit. Meanwhile the dance routines of stars like Britney Spears and Christina Aguilera, which our little girls are so keen to copy, are little more than slickly produced stripper routines, based on the maximum exposure of crotch, cleavage, and buttocks. While the pop stars of the past modestly kept their legs together, crotch displays and buttock thrusting, jiggling, or shaking are now the most common dance moves. Today's pop videos show pop stars as porn stars, as women constantly ready for sex. In case there is any confusion, in the song lyrics women are referred to as ho's and sluts. Some of the hottest video directors are hired from porn movies.

Women are there mainly for decoration. The British Home Office report into the sexualization of young people found that half of the women in music videos don't sing or play an instrument. They are treated as objects. As the psychologist Linda Papadopoulos points out, whereas men are shown as "hyper-masculine and sexually dominant", women are often depicted as being "in a state of sexual readiness".[85] Of course, from Elvis to James Brown and the Rolling Stones, music and sex have always been inextricably linked. Somehow because it's "rock'n'roll", video makers get away with more. But really they don't deserve to. They can't claim they don't know what they are doing, because their biggest consumers are young people. Yet a study of MTV's content by the Parents' Television Council in the USA found 1,548 sexual scenes containing 3,056 depictions of sex or nudity in just seventy-one hours. That's a sexual scene every 6.6 minutes.[86]

What you can do:

Set limits. Explain that just because rude lyrics are set to music, they still mean something and it doesn't make it all right to sing them.

Turn off the X-rated soundtrack. Of all the influences discussed here, music videos are the easiest to avoid. Don't leave video channels on all day, and set your teenager daughter's parental controls to stop her downloading them. Ask entertainers not to play inappropriately adult music at children's parties and discos. Think twice about mindlessly switching on pop music radio stations in the car during the school run – or you may end up shocked by some of the words you hear repeated back.

Watch videos with them. With older girls, point out how women are used as sex objects and decoration, while men are usually shown as powerful and in control.

Offer better musical role models. Instead of letting them grow up on a diet of scantily dressed, manufactured girl bands, try introducing CDs by strong, independent singer song-writers such as Kate Bush, Annie Lennox, Björk, and Ellie Goulding.

Engaged – doing what? How to help your daughter use mobile phones safely

"The single most important possession in my life is my mobile. I use it for everything and I'd be totally lost without it. I keep everyone up to date on Twitter and I can use the internet to see what's going on in the world. I also use it as my diary and my radio. It's my whole world."
Samantha, 13

Remember the days when you had to ask your parents for permission to use the big clunky household phone? Not only was the clock ticking on how long you talked for, it was also probably in the hall, where the whole family could listen to every word. And of course, all you could do back then was speak and be spoken to, unlike today's gadgets which are TV, internet, camera, and everything else rolled into one tiny, mobile package.

There is no denying how much easier mobiles have made our lives. Every mother I spoke to had given her daughter a mobile phone, almost as a rite of passage, before she went to secondary school. Even though they grew up safely without them, parents are often insistent that mobiles are necessary because of the perceived dangers of allowing their girls to be out in the wide world alone. Girls also push for them initially to keep in touch with their parents – and as a way to be allowed more independence, especially as phones are the most visible peer group possession of all.

All of this means that mobile phones occupy a difficult place in modern parenthood. Of all the technology that surrounds our children, they are the most difficult moving targets for parents to keep tabs on. Although many parents start off giving their girls the most basic models, fearing they will lose them, over time phones rapidly get upgraded to include internet access.

It's then that phones become hand-held computers, portals to every conceivable message and image. According to the UK Department for Children, Schools, and Families, 91 per cent of children aged twelve to seventeen have their own mobile phone and 12 per cent say they use it to access the internet.[87]

The risks of this are just the same as with a computer. Many girls' first exposure to pornography is through unwelcome picture messages that pop up on their mobile screens. Because phones are by their very nature "mobile" and "personal", it's easier for girls to evade monitoring if they want to. Mothers I spoke to who thought they'd turned off the internet at night found their daughters using their mobiles to get on to Facebook under the bedclothes.

Camera phones can tempt girls to take pictures they may regret, or pass on without thinking. Ill-considered texts, fired off in the heat of the moment, are also a major cause of flare-ups, misunderstandings, and rows with friends. One in fifteen children aged eleven to thirteen says they have received nasty or threatening text messages. Mobile phones are also becoming the most popular medium for viewing music videos. Four out of ten teenagers surveyed have video downloading capability on their mobile phones. Among these teenagers, music videos are the most watched type of material for nearly seven out of ten.[88]

What you can do:

FOR YOUNGER GIRLS:
Don't use mobiles to keep them entertained. Now there are a multitude of applications and video games on our mobiles, many parents use phones like a dummy for kids to keep them quiet. Resist this if you can. Otherwise the demand for their own phone will start even earlier, because they'll see phones primarily as toys.

Switch on the controls before you hand it over. These days it's very easy to download adult content on most phones. But, according to a recent British government report, nine out of ten parents fail to contact the mobile phone company to turn on the inbuilt safety measures that are fitted to most models. If you don't want your child spending too much time on social networking sites, some phone companies can filter those out too.[89]

Make her first phone a family phone. For as long as possible, give her a family mobile phone that everyone uses, so she practises borrowing it and can prove she can use it responsibly.

Buy the simplest handset. The younger the child, the simpler the phone. In any case most young people will lose their first few models.

Check your phone use around your kids. If you are constantly using your mobile when you are with your children, or are texting at the supper table instead of finding out how their day has gone, what example are you setting? Few emails or texts are that important. Ask yourself if the call or message can wait until after their bedtime.

FOR OLDER GIRLS:
Warn her about text bullying. Once, we could leave school bullying behind as soon as we shut the front door. But these days mobile phones mean that nasty messages can follow your child wherever she goes. Warn her how common text bullying is, so she is better able to cope and doesn't see it as something that is only happening to her.

Teach her the language of texting. Because texting seems like a form of disembodied communication, teach her that her words may be seen out of context and be read as nastier than she meant them to be. Tell her to only send the sort of texts she would like to get. Warn her that what might seem like an in-joke – such as calling her friend a slut by text – can be taken extremely seriously by a friend's parent if they see it, and cause all sorts of trouble. Also warn her that the speed and immediacy of texting might tempt her to make an inappropriate comment before she's thought about the consequences.

Draw up the rules together from the start. Make it clear you are buying a phone as a safety tool, not a status symbol. Explain that rules about using it are there to keep her safe. Agree between you that if she doesn't abide by them then she may lose phone privileges. Unless your daughter is cyber-bullying, don't confiscate it completely, as a phone is a teenager's lifeline. But do consider reducing talk plans or cutting off features.

Make her phone her responsibility. To stop use getting out of control, make your child responsible for her own phone by asking her to finance a "pay-as-you-go" plan out of her own pocket money. Many children, however, will play up to this and use lack of credit as an excuse to be unavailable. Charlie Taylor, who is head of a London special school, recommends making it a rule that teenagers are not allowed to leave the house without a topped-up phone.

Ban texting during homework, meals, and conversations. Make it clear to your daughter that eye-to-eye interaction and conversation have priority over texts. Explain that it's not enough for her just to be in the room.

Consider checking software. Some mobile phone companies will allow you to view the numbers your child is ringing by logging on to your computer. It may not be a bad thing to let her know there are restraints.

Tell her never to upload risqué pictures. Now that most mobiles take pictures too, talk to your child about what it's not appropriate to photograph and circulate, no matter how daring or funny it seems at the time. Give her examples of girls who have been humiliated by pictures and videos going viral on mobile phones and the internet. Explain that once she's sent an image, anyone can forward it, and there's nothing she do to get it back.

Turn off Bluetooth. Bluetooth means that your child can be contacted by any other Bluetooth users nearby – so switch it off.

Give her a healthy respect for the technology: The jury is still out on whether a rise in brain tumours is down to more mobile phone use among young people. Certainly the scientists point to the fact that phone radio waves are likely to travel more easily into the brain of young people because their skulls are still thickening, and their brains are composed of more water and are less dense. Graham Philips, a spokesman for the safety lobby group Powerwatch, said: "Most people in the UK have no idea that government advice is that under-sixteens don't use their phones. Public information is sorely lacking." For that reason, it may not hurt to remind her that it's possible that having her phone glued to her skull might not be the best idea. Indeed mobile phones are to be banned in French primary schools, and operators must offer handsets that allow only text messages.[90]

Quizzes and games

One of the simplest and most enjoyable ways to prolong your daughter's childhood is to play with her. Rather than leaving her to play solitary games on her computer or allowing her life to be taken over by fashion or make-up, give her the companionship and interaction of board games and quizzes.

Star cards. This is a box of fifty-two cards, with descriptions such as loving, patient, and honest, which help children get to know themselves and recognize their inner qualities (www. relax.kids.com).

The awkward question game. Get communication going by asking each other tricky questions – and answering honestly so you get to know each other better.

Mind-mapping. This is a great idea adapted from the concept invented by Tony Buzan. Get your daughter to draw herself or write her name in the middle of a page and link up all the things that are important about her. You may find at first that she defines herself by the toys and gadgets she owns. Instead show her how to think of herself in terms of the qualities she possesses, such as humour and loyalty.

Talk about each other's childhoods. Few things are more intriguing to a daughter than when you share stories about your own experiences as a child. Tell her about how your childhood compares with or differs from her own.

Play "Would You Rather?". Make up a string of funny dilemmas such as "Would you rather be the queen of England or the prime minister?" to help her stretch her imagination and think about her priorities.

Argue with your daughter. Choose a topic to debate. It helps girls to see an argument from both sides, form their opinions, and see that a difference of view doesn't have to lead to a row.

Let your daughter play outdoors. Just five minutes' "green exercise" can make your child feel better about herself, according to a study from the University of Essex. By letting children get to grips with nature, you help them see themselves in the context of the greater world. Climbing trees also teaches children how to take responsibility and measure risk.

Build a family tree. Teach your child about roots. Make it real for her by drawing your family tree and adding photographs of ancestors to the branches.

Make a time capsule. Show girls how they can put together some of the things that are important to them here and now. Collect objects such as photos, a newspaper cutting, and notes about their likes and dislikes. Then seal it in a safe place and open it in five years' time.

The Art of Conversation cards. This is a set of 100 conversation builders for kids which can help you find out their opinions on subjects you may never have asked them about. Go to www.taoc.com.au.

Make a "Me collage". Help girls think about who they are and what they like by cutting out pictures of the things they value and making a collage which sums up who they are and what interests them.

Put together a treasure box. One of the most meaningful gifts a child can have is a keepsake box. Let her fill it with christening or naming day gifts, heirlooms, special mementos, or cards. A child will go back to it again and again and it will help her to remember how treasured and loved she is.

"Want to play sexy ladies?" Guiding your daughter towards healthy toys and games for her age

"My friend plays with Barbies but then she cut all their hair off and threw them in the bin. I don't like them either. It looks funny that she's got a child's face on the body of a lady with boobs."
Tasha, 6

"My daughter loves Bratz dolls. She likes their style and they have really funky clothes. I think it's a really clever idea. She role-plays them competing in X-Factor and going in for competitions."
Michelle, 34

A visit to the dolls aisle at Toys "R" Us is a bracing lesson in what our little girls are supposed to be interested in these days. Dolls are essential to child development because they help children to see their own place in the world and learn the different roles people play. But if their playthings are anything to go by, our children can look forward to a life in hooker clothing and high heels, with a mobile phone glued to one hand and a powder compact in the other.

Step back and if you can adjust your eyes to the blinding sugar pink around you, think about the messages these toys are sending to girls. Unless the dolls are wearing skinny jeans, there is not one dressed in a skirt which reaches below the top of their spindly plastic thighs. Compared to her successors, the Bratz and Moxie Girls ranges, Barbie now looks like a natural beauty. With their inflated lips and big hair, Bratz in particular looked like scaled-down sex dolls. When it came to providing the dolls with something to do, there were some accessories such as horses and skateboards. But these were massively outnumbered by pink hair-dryers, miniature handbags, and manicure sets. Children's potential to develop is greatly narrowed when even their playthings are stereotyped in this way. Don't our daughters deserve better than to learn about life through these plastic caricatures of modern womanhood?

What you can do:

Don't buy dolls with cleavage. Let your little girls be children by buying them dolls that are children too. Then, instead of loading her dollies up with pink mobiles and make-up kits, let your daughter decide what games she wants to play with her toys. Look for playthings that are less sexual, such as stuffed animals or rag dolls.

Talk about what dolls do. If your little girl just loves Barbies, Moxies, or Bratz, discuss what she likes about them. Ask her if she's ever met a woman who looks like one in real life. Tell her all the things that Barbie wouldn't be able to do if she was a real woman because her feet are arched permanently for high heels. Suggest games where Barbie becomes a scientist or a politician.

Buy basic toys. Don't buy toys linked to movie franchises where the scripts are already written. Allow your children to use their imagination to create their own play world. Stick with the basics by buying them simple playthings so they have to use their creativity.

Conclusion

As I write, both porn and prostitution have become mainstream in our culture, even aspirational. On television, more than a million people have been glued to every episode of *Secret Diary of a Call Girl* in which Billie Piper pays a high-class sex worker with an enviable lifestyle of walk-in wardrobes packed with Manolo Blahnik shoes.

"Why do I do it?" challenges her character Belle brazenly. "I love sex and money. I'm lazy. I'm my own boss. I love the anonymity. I'm the expensively dressed woman you see gliding across the hotel lobby – fabulous but forgettable." Lest we wonder why Belle sells her body to be used for sex, she adds the justification: "It's better than watching the clock until the next scheduled tea break."

During the commercial breaks, an ad recently featured a well-spoken young woman in her twenties driving in a car with her mother. The younger woman winces as they pass a billboard advertising her services as a stripper. Approvingly, her parent remarks: "You never told me you'd got a job."

No wonder, in the midst of all this, one middle-market national newspaper ran a feature this week headlined: "How did the world's oldest profession become a career choice for middle-class girls?"

It's also a measure of how far we've come that "slut" has now been reclaimed as a term of praise. I came across one sixteen-year-old girl at a top public school who was so proud of the term she had it spelled out in giant letters as her phone screensaver.

It's telling too that while more women in this country go to university than ever before, our female graduates aren't raving about the opportunities opening up to them in politics or business. Instead some of our cleverest young women feel the need to court publicity by posing nude, entering beauty contests, and filling vacancies in the sex industry. According to research by the University of Leeds, one in four lap dancers now has a degree.[91]

As Charlotte Litten, aged twenty-four, who has a foundation degree in media and journalism, explains without embarrassment: "Lap dancing is the perfect way to earn money while you are studying. The hours are flexible and it's better paid than waitressing."[92]

Meanwhile the Cambridge University magazine *Varsity* has just featured its first nude modelling shots of female students, despite the fact that not so long ago their mothers would have had to fight hard for admission to male colleges.[93] Up and down the country, female students line up to parade for university beauty pageants.

While it is of course a woman's right to choose her own path, in any era before this such aspirations to be sex objects would have been unthinkable. But sleaze has become so acceptable it's become normal in the world our children inhabit too. What have our younger children got to look up to when their big sisters have been seduced by the belief that stupidity makes you sexier?

The liberation of women promised our little girls that they could grow up to do anything and everything. Instead that promise has been corrupted into the message that girls can and should do anything and everything when having sex.

As parents, what signals are we sending our daughters when we barely even raise an eyebrow? In the past, magazines and TV programmes were careful not to step over the line because they feared a parental backlash. But because we have worried it would look "uncool", "right wing", or "anti free speech", we've said nothing and done nothing for so long that few dare speak up.

In the years to come, I hope we will look back at this post-internet period in the same way as we once viewed children being sent down mines and up chimneys after the industrial revolution. Just as the unregulated labour practices of the Victorian era robbed those boys and girls of their childhoods, so is sexualization and a free-for-all raunch culture robbing our daughters of theirs.

As it stands, our girls are already being choked by the expectations on them, while we do no more than send a canary down the mine-shaft to try and guess how bad it's going to get. Our daughters have had the hard-won freedom to grow into who and what they want to be taken from them. They have learned they will only be popular at school, be seen as all-round successes and win the attention and admiration of men if they fit into a very narrow stereotype of female attractiveness and success.

Instead of enjoying the carefree days of childhood, they feel they have no choice but to spend this precious time working out a way to fit into this hierarchy. Our children are forced to live in a vacuous world where looks are all that matter to them – because that's all that seems to matter to other people.

From the publication of *Lolita* in the 1950s and the sexualization of models like Brooke Shields in the 1980s, of course it's nothing new to shock, and grab attention by turning children into sex objects. But they were one-offs which caused huge storms of outrage at the time.

What's different now is that we face a perfect storm, where celebrity, porn culture and consumerism have come together into a whirlwind that parents feel unable – and sometimes even reluctant – to withstand.

I wholeheartedly support the government's latest reviews looking at how to curb the sexualization of children, and stamp out the easy accessibility of free pornography. But as the most important role model for our children, the best thing we can do for them is to reclaim our positions as the first gatekeepers in their lives – and turn the tide again so our daughters can be children, not trainee sex objects. Our aim should be to make it as tasteless to hold makeover parties for little girls or to sell them high heels as it has now become to buy them cigarette shaped sweets and toy guns.

Whether or not you agree with the conclusions of this book, for me there's one incontrovertible fact that shows it's all gone too far. Such is the sex industry's fascination with the corruption of innocence that the trend now is for adult women to shave off their pubic hair to look like children again. The fact that it's now mainstream fashion for most women I know illustrates how acceptable it has become to blur the lines between adulthood and childhood. Deep down, I believe society still knows that children should be protected. It's now up to us as parents to pull together and remind marketers, legislators, TV channel bosses, and the internet service providers – as well as support the first legislative steps towards taking the matter in hand. But the first step is to remind ourselves.

Resources

Book resources

Terri Apter, *The Confident Child*, New York: W. W. Norton and Co, 1997.

Laura Berman, *Sex Ed*, London: Dorling Kindersley, 2009.

Pat Craven, *Living with the Dominator*, Knighton: Freedom Publishing, 2008.

JoAnn Deak with Teresa Barker, *Girls Will Be Girls: Raising Confident and Courageous Daughters*, New York: Hyperion, 2002.

Gail Dines, *Pornland*, Boston: Beacon Press, 2010.

M. G. Durham, *The Lolita Effect*, London: Gerald Duckworth & Co, 2009.

David Dutwin, *Unplug Your Kids*, Avon, MA: Adams Media, 2009.

Jeanne and Don Elium, *Raising a Daughter*, California: Celestial Arts, 2003.

Ian and Mary Grant, *Raising Confident Girls*, London: Vermilion, 2009.

Maggie Hamilton, *What's Happening to Our Girls?* Camberwell, Victoria: Viking, 2008.

Elizabeth Hartley-Brewer, *Self-Esteem for Girls*, London: Vermilion, 2000.

Noel Janis-Norton, *Could Do Better*, Edinburgh: Barrington Stoke, 2005.

Erika V. Shearin Karres, *Mean Chicks, Cliques and Dirty Tricks*, Avon, MA: Adams Media, 2004.

Alfie Kohn, *Unconditional Parenting*, New York: Atria Books, 2005.

Richard Layard and Judy Dunn, *A Good Childhood: Searching for Values in a Competitive Age*, London: Penguin, 2009.

Diane E. Levin and Jean Kilbourne, *So Sexy, So Soon*, New York: Ballantine Books, 2008.

Ariel Levy, *Female Chauvinist Pigs*, London: Pocket Books, 2005.

Gael Lindenfield, *Confident Children*, London: Thorsons, 2001.

Ed Mayo and Agnes Nairn, *Consumer Kids*, London: Constable and Robinson, 2009.

Sue Palmer, *Detoxing Childhood*, London: Orion, 2007.

Rob Parsons, *The Sixty Minute Family*, Oxford: Lion, 2010.

Pamela Paul, *Pornified: How Pornography is Damaging Our Lives, Our Relationships and Our Families*, New York: Holt, 2005.

Gisela Preuschoff, *Raising Girls*, London: Harper Thorsons, 2005.

C. J. Simister, *The Bright Stuff*, Harlow: Pearson Education, 2008.

Melinda Tankard Reist (ed.), *Getting Real: Challenging the Sexualisation of Girls*, Melbourne: Spinifex Press, 2009.

Natasha Walter, *Living Dolls: The Return of Sexism*, London: Virago, 2010.
Rosalind Wiseman, *Queen Bees and Wannabes*, New York: Three Rivers Press, 2002.

Books for girls

John Burningham, *Would You Rather?* London: Red Fox, 1994. This clever book is great for helping kids to get to know themselves by weighing up alternatives.

Chris David, Erin Falligant, and Stacy Peterson, *Just Mom and Me*, Middleton, WI: American Girl Publishing, 2008. This and others in the American Girl series help mums, daughters, and families understand each other better through quizzes and activities.

David Fontana, *Nightlights: Stories for You to Read to Your Child to Encourage Calm, Confidence and Creativity*, London: Duncan Baird Publishers, 2003. A calming book for bedtime, which helps kids visualize positive messages.

Tamra Wight and Ross Collins, *The Three Grumpies*, New York: Bloomsbury, 2003. This picture book tells the story of a little girl who learns to name and deal with her emotions – and get rid of the negative thoughts in her head.

Internet resources

www.ceop.police.uk – Child Exploitation and Online Protection Centre
www.careforthefamily.org.uk
www.commonsensemedia.org
www.faithandfreedom.webs.com – Natalie Collins
www.fundamentalsonline.co.uk
www.mediawatchuk.org.uk
www.pinkstinks.co.uk
www.pogopack.co.uk – Pogo packs: positively preparing girls for puberty
www.safefamilies.org
www.calmerparenting.co.uk – Calmer, Easier, Happier Parenting

Acknowledgments

With many thanks to all the following, as well as the many mums and daughters who shared their experiences with me:
Noel Janis-Norton at Calmer, Easier, Happier Parenting, Michelle Garcia Winner, Dr Amanda Gummer, Kate Kirkpatrick, Deanne Jade, Professor Julia Buckroyd, Sonia Ducie, Hilary Freeman, Mili Harwood, Carly Silver, Teresa Dunbar, Pat Craven, Natalie Collins, Anthony Harwood, Lily and Clio Harwood, Tara Carey, Robyn and Amy West, Becca and Ambur, Rob Parsons, Anne Dellaporta, Shari Robinson, Dr Nollaig Fenn, Raymond Francis, Jason Dean, Kate Harwood, and Claudia Redmond.

Endnotes

1. Anita Singh, "Fit for a Lap Dancer: The Heels on Sale for Girls Age Three", *Daily Telegraph* (14 June 2010).

2. Jenny Johnston, "Mummy's Little Lolita", *Daily Mail* (8 July 2008).

3. See the Mental Health Foundation, www.mentalhealth.org.uk.

4. Richard Layard and Judy Dunn, *A Good Childhood: Searching for Values in a Competitive Age*, London: Penguin, 2009.

5. Mintel International Group Ltd, *Cosmetic Surgery – UK*, June 2010.

6. Mintel, *Cosmetic Surgery – UK*.

7. Natasha Courtenay-Smith, "What are Their Mothers Thinking?", *Daily Mail* (30 May 2009).

8. Diana Appleyard, "Primary School Prom Queens", *Daily Mail* (16 July 2010).

9. Interview with Kirsty Gallacher, GMTV, August 2010, available at http://www.youtube.com/watch?v=MRd9LU1CvzA.

10. Rachel Porter, "Portrait of a Very Modern 14-year-old", *Daily Mail* (18 November 2010).

11. Mothers' Union report, *Bye Buy Childhood*, September 2010.

12. Heidi Blake, "Padded Bras for Girls, 9, on the Shelves at Asda; Store Removes Items After Complaint from Mother Over Sexual Abuse Risk", *Daily Telegraph* (12 October 2010).

13. D. Kirby, "Emerging Answers 2007: New Research Findings on Programs to Reduce Teen Pregnancy", at http://www.thenationalcampaign.org/resources/pdf/pubs/EA2007_FINAL.pdf.

14. Sonia Livingstone and Magdalena Bober, "UK Children Go Online: Final Report of Key Project Findings", London: LSE, 2005.

15. Claire McAteer, "I Want, by Pole-dancing Girl, 6, to Become a Glamour Model", *Closer* (26 June 2010). Dulcie Pearce, "Only hypocrites criticize my parenting", *The Sun* (16 June 2010).

16. Nancy Etcoff, Susie Orbach, Jennifer Scott, and Heidi D'Agostino, *The Real Truth About Beauty*: Findings of the Global Study on Women, Beauty and Well-Being, 2004.

17. A. Burgess, "The Costs and Benefits of Active Fatherhood: Evidence and Insights to Inform the Development of Policy and Practice", and C. Lewis and M. Lamb, *Fatherhood: Connecting the Strands of Diversity across Time and Space*, cited in Layard and Dunn, *A Good Childhood*.

18. Robyn Dixon, "Parental Influences on the Dieting Beliefs and Behaviors of Adolescent Females in New Zealand", *Journal of Adolescent Health*, 19/4 (1996).

19. Ian and Mary Grant, *Raising Confident Girls*, London: Vermilion, 2009.

20. Diane E. Levin and Jean Kilbourne, *So Sexy, So Soon*, New York: Ballantine Books, 2008.

21. See Gisela Preuschoff, *Raising Girls*, London: Harper Thorsons, 2005.

22. Layard and Dunn, *A Good Childhood*.

23. Rob Parsons, *The Sixty Minute Family*, Oxford: Lion, 2010.

24. Layard and Dunn, *A Good Childhood*.

25. Robert J. Sternberg, S*uccessful Intelligence: How Practical and Creative Intelligence Determine Success in Life*, New York: Plume, 1997, and Howard Gardner, *Frames of Mind: The Theory of Multiple Intelligences*, New York: Basic Books, 1993.

26. Interview with the author.

27. Calmer, Easier, Happier Parenting, www.calmerparenting.co.uk.

28. Stephen R. Covey, *The 7 Habits of Highly Effective People*, London: Simon and Schuster, 1989.

29. JoAnn Deak with Teresa Barker, *Girls Will Be Girls: Raising Confident and Courageous Daughters*, New York: Hyperion, 2002.

30. Michael Grose at www.parentingideas.com.au, and "Eating Dinner at the Table is 'Dying Out'", *Daily Mail* (12 April 2010).

31. Linda Papadopoulos, *Sexualisation of Young People Review*, London: Home Office, 2010.

32. See the "Put Pornography in its Place" campaign, *Psychologies*, July 2010, http://www.psychologies.co.uk/put-pornography-in-its-place/.

33. Livingstone and Bober, "UK Children Go Online".

34. Gail Dines, *Pornland*, Boston: Beacon Press, 2010.

35. Dines, *Pornland*.

36. Survey for Channel 4's *The Sex Education Show v. Pornography*, March 2009.

37. John Henly, "Let's Talk About Sex: Repressed? Hardly. The Most Comprehensive Survey of American Sex Lives in 20 Years Reveals What's Really Going on in Bed", *The Guardian* (6 October 2010), citing National Health and Social Life Survey, University of Chicago, 1988.

38. Leslie Scrivener, "As Australia Ponders Tough Online Censorship Laws, Research on Internet Pornography and Teen Sexuality Suggests the Kids Might Be All Right", *Toronto Star* (17 January 2009).

39. Jochen Peter and Patti M. Valkenburg, *Adolescents' Exposure to Sexually*

Explicit Internet Material, Sexual Uncertainty, and Attitudes Toward Uncommitted Sexual Exploration, Amsterdam: University of Amsterdam, 2008.

40. Attorney General's Commission on Pornography, for US Attorney General Edwin Meese, 1986. Survey for Channel 4's *The Sex Education Show v. Pornography*.

41. Patricia M. Greenfield, "Inadvertent Exposure to Pornography on the Internet: Implications of Peer-to-peer File-sharing Networks for Child Development and Families", *Applied Developmental Psychology* 25 (2004).

42. Pamela Paul, *Pornified*, New York: Holt, 2005.

43. Gary Brooks, *The Centrefold Syndrome*, Hoboken, NJ: Jossey Bass, 1995.

44. Dick Thornburgh and Herbert S. Lin (eds), *Youth, Pornography, and the Internet*, Washington: National Academy Press, 2002.

45. Steven C. Martino, "Beyond the 'Big Talk': The Roles of Breadth and Repetition in Parent–Adolescent Communication About Sexual Topics", *Pediatrics*, 122/3 (March 2008).

46. Sarah Womack, "British Youngsters Get the Worst Deal", *Daily Telegraph* (14 February 2007).

47. Layard and Dunn, *A Good Childhood*.

48. Rosalind Wiseman, *Queen Bees and Wannabes*, New York: Three Rivers Press, 2002.

49. Wiseman, *Queen Bees and Wannabes*.

50. Wiseman, *Queen Bees and Wannabes*.

51. J. M. Gottman, "The Observation of Social Process", cited in Layard and Dunn, *A Good Childhood*.

52. David Nelson, "Aversive Parenting in China: Associations with Child Physical and Relational Aggression", *Child Development*, 77/3 (May/June 2006).

53. Interview with the author.

54. "Key Children's Sites Adopt ClickCEOP Button as UK's Centre for Child Protection Receives Over 6,000 Reports in a Year", http://www.ceop.police.uk/Media-Centre/Press-releases/2010/, (5 November 2010).

55. Papadopoulos, *Sexualisation of Young People Review*.

56. McAfee and Harris Interactive, "The Secret Online Lives of Teens", June 2010, at http://us.mcafee.com/en-us/local/docs/lives_of_teens.pdf.

57. Martin Lindström with Patricia B. Seybold, *BRANDchild: Remarkable Insights in the Minds of Today's Global Kids and Their Relationships with Brands*, London: Kogan Page, 2003.

58. David Piachaud, "Freedom to Be a Child: Commercial Pressures on

Children", London: Centre for Analysis of Social Exclusion, London School of Economics and Political Science, 2007, at http://eprints.lse.ac.uk/6206/.

59. "The Commercialisation of Childhood", London: Compass, 2006, at http://www.compassonline.org.uk/publications/.

60. Sharon Beder, *This Little Kiddy Went to Market: The Corporate Capture of Childhood: The Corporate Assault on Children*, London: Pluto Press, 2009.

61. Richard Elliott and Claire Leonard, "Peer Pressures and Poverty", *Journal of Consumer Behaviour*, 3/4 (2004).

62. "Teenage Gear", online survey commissioned by Esure via Onepoll, which interviewed a random sample of 3,000 parents between 14 and 18 December 2009, at http://www.onepoll.com/press-archive/teens-own-5k-of-stuff.

63. Sue Palmer, *Toxic Childhood*, London: Orion, 2007.

64. Ed Mayo and Agnes Nairn, *Consumer Kids*, London: Constable and Robinson, 2009.

65. Interview with the author.

66. Papadopoulos, *Sexualisation of Young People Review*.

67. http://www.mumsnet.com/campaigns/let-girls-be-girls.

68. Diana Appleyard, "Primary School Prom Queens", *Daily Mail* (16 July 2010).

69.Samantha Rose, "Trends in Tween Cosmetics", 2 May 2008, at http://www.fashionindustrytoday.com/2008/05/02/trends-in-tween-cosmetics.

70. Douglas Quenqua, "Graduating from Lip Smackers", *New York Times* (29 April 2010), citing market research by NPD.

71. Stacey Tantleff-Dunn and Sharon Hayes, "Am I Too Fat to Be a Princess? Examining the Effects of Popular Children's Media on Young Girls' Body Image", *British Journal of Developmental Psychology*, 28/2 (June 2010).

72. Psychology experiment for *London Tonight*, November 2009. For the experiment, more than 100 women aged between thirty-five and seventy were instructed to spend a week carrying a special counter that they had to click each time they had a negative thought about their faces or bodies, or themselves in general. On average, the women clicked their devices thirty-six times every day. That is a total of 252 negative thoughts in a week.

73. Interview with the author.

74. Interview with the author.

75. Interview with the author.

76. Interview with the author.

77. Girlguiding UK, "Girls' Attitudes Survey", 2009, at http://girlsattitudes.girlguiding.org.uk/home.aspx.

78. Daniel Clay, Vivian L. Vignoles, and Helga Dittmar, "Body Image and

Self-Esteem Among Adolescent Girls: Testing the Influence of Sociocultural Factors", *Journal of Research on Adolescence*, 15 (2005).

79. Emma Rush and Andrea La Nauze, *Letting Children Be Children – Stopping the Sexualisation of Children in Australia*, Manuka: Australia Institute, 2006.

80. American Psychological Association, "Violence in the Media – Psychologists Help Protect Children from Harmful Effects", at www.apa.org/research/action/protect.asp

81. Aric Sigman, "How Superskinny TV Stars are Harming Our Health", *Daily Mail* (18 October 2010).

82. Study Conducted by RAND Corporation and published in *Pediatrics* (September 2004).

83. BBC Healthy Britain Poll, a nationwide phone poll of 1,010 adults in England, Wales, and Scotland conducted by ICM between 20 and 22 August 2004.

84. Mayo and Nairn, *Consumer Kids*.

85. Papadopoulos, *Sexualisation of Young People Review*.

86. Casey Williams, "MTV Smut Peddlers: Targeting Kids with Sex, Drugs and Alcohol: A Report on MTV Programming", March 2004, at http://www.parentstv.org/ptc/publications/reports/mtv2005/main.asp.

87. Tanya Byron, "Do We Have Safer Children in a Digital World? A Review of Progress Since the 2008 Byron Review", at http://www.dcsf.gov.uk/byronreview/pdfs/do%20we%20have%20safer%20children%20in%20a%20digital%20world-WEB.pdf.

88. Byron, "Do We Have Safer Children?"

89. Byron, "Do We Have Safer Children?"

90. Peter Allen and Fiona McRae, "French Drive to Stop Young Using Mobiles", *Daily Mail* (12 January 2009).

91. Heidi Blake, "One in Four Lap Dancers Has a Degree", *Daily Telegraph* (27 August 2010).

92. Interview, *Reveal* magazine (August 2010).

93. "Student Charlotte Makes History by Posing Topless", *Cambridge Evening News* (24 November 2010).

Index